Horse Owner's Concise Guide

by

Elsie V. Hanauer

1973 EDITION

Published by

W ILSHIRE BOOK COMPANY
12015 Sherman Road
No. Hollywood, California 91605
Telephone: (213) 875-1711

Library of Congress Catalogue Card Number: 69-14880

A. S. Barnes and Co.
Cranbury, New Jersey 08512

Thomas Yoseloff Ltd
108 New Bond Street
London W1Y OQX, England

First printing March, 1969
Second printing March, 1970

Printed by
HAL LEIGHTON PRINTING CO.
P. O. Box 1231
Beverly Hills, California 90213
Telephone: (213) 346-8500

SBN: 498-06970-2
Printed in the United States of America

Contents

Horse Owner's Concise Guide

Conformation

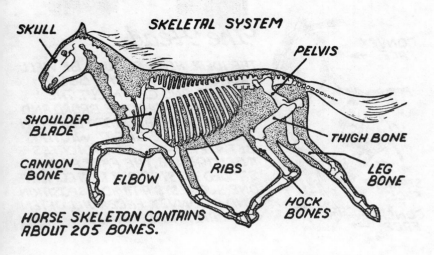

SKELETAL SYSTEM

SKULL

PELVIS

SHOULDER BLADE

THIGH BONE

CANNON BONE

ELBOW

RIBS

LEG BONE

HOCK BONES

HORSE SKELETON CONTAINS ABOUT 205 BONES.

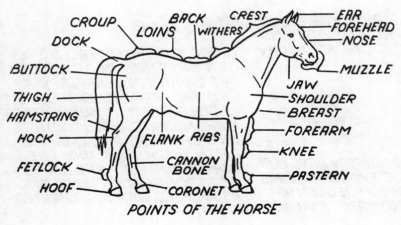

CROUP

BACK

CREST

EAR

FOREHEAD

LOINS

WITHERS

NOSE

DOCK

BUTTOCK

MUZZLE

THIGH

JAW

HAMSTRING

SHOULDER

BREAST

HOCK

FOREARM

FLANK

RIBS

KNEE

FETLOCK

CANNON BONE

HOOF

PASTERN

CORONET

POINTS OF THE HORSE

11

The Head

CONVEX FACE.

STRAIGHT FACE.

CONCAVE FACE.

THE IDEAL HEAD SHOULD BE WELL PROPORTIONED TO THE BODY, REFINED AND CLEAN CUT. THE FOREHEAD SHOULD BE BROAD AND FULL WITH GREAT WIDTH BETWEEN THE EYES. THE GREAT WIDTH BETWEEN THE EYES INDICATES INTELLIGENCE. THE FACE PROFILE SHOULD BE STRAIGHT AS A CONCAVE ONE SUGGESTS A TIMID DISPOSITION AND A CONVEX FACE WILL OFTEN INDICATE STUBBORNESS.

The Eye

SCARS ON THE EYELIDS ARE UNSIGHTLY AND INDICATE AN INJURY

WHICH MAY HAVE LEFT THE EYE WEAK. TEARS SHED FREQUENTLY INDICATE A WEAK EYE.

LARGE, FULL, WELL PLACED EYES OF A CHESTNUT HUGE COLOR ARE BEAUTIFUL IN APPEARANCE AND THEY ARE THE LEAST SUBJECT TO DISEASE. SMALL, SUNKEN EYES MAY INDICATE A SLUGGISH TEMPERAMENT AND THEY ARE OFTEN WEAK. EYES THAT ARE VERY PROMINENT ARE APT TO BE STRONGLY CONVEXED AND ASSOCIATED WITH NEARSIGHTED-NESS.

NOSTRILS CONSTANTLY
DISTENDED AND HARD
MAY INDICATE HEAVES.

THE LIPS
SHOULD BE FIRM.

The Muzzle

THE NOSTRILS SHOULD BE LARGE
AND PLIABLE WITH THE INSIDE A
ROSE COLOR AT REST AND DEEP
RED DURING EXERCISE. IF THE
LOWER LIP IS NOT HELD FIRMLY
AGAINST THE UPPER LIP IT MAY
BE DUE TO A LACK OF VIGOR. ANY
SCARS LEFT ON THE UPPER LIP
FROM THE FREQUENT USE OF A
TWITCH COULD INDICATE A
HORSE WITH BAD HABITS.

The Chest

THE CHEST SHOULD BE WIDE
ENOUGH TO PROVIDE AMPLE ROOM
FOR THE HEART AND LUNGS. A
WIDE CHEST INDICATES A STRONG
CONSTITUTION, BUT EXCESSIVE
WIDTH IN THE CHEST SETS THE
FORELEGS TOO NEAR THE OUTSIDE
AND AS A RESULT THE HORSE IS
LIABLE TO PADDLE WITH HIS FRONT
FEET.

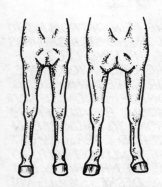

CHEST TOO   CHEST TOO
NARROW.   WIDE.

13

CONFORMATION OF FORELEGS

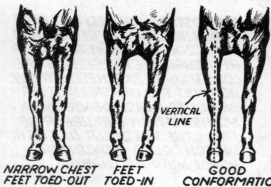

WHEN VIEWED FROM THE FRONT, A VERTICAL LINE FROM THE POINT OF THE SHOULDER SHOULD BISECT ALL THE REGIONS OF THE LEG. THE CHEST SHOULD BE OF MODERATE BREADTH TO PROVIDE AMPLE ROOM FOR THE VITAL ORGANS OF BREATHING.

NARROW CHEST FEET TOED-OUT

VERTICAL LINE

FEET TOED-IN

GOOD CONFORMATION

CONFORMATION OF HIND LEGS

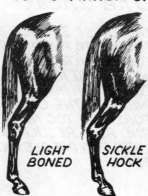

THE LENGTH FROM HIP TO HOCK AND STRAIGHTNESS OF THE HIND LEGS ARE FACTORS WHICH MAKE FOR SPEED AND GOOD CONFORMATION. THE HOCK SHOULD BE WIDE FROM FRONT TO BACK, CLEAN CUT AND CORRECTLY SET. THE HIND FEET TEND TO TOE OUT NATURALLY, BUT THE DEGREE SHOULD NOT BE TOO GREAT.

GOOD LEG

LIGHT BONED

SICKLE HOCK

Hindquarters

GOOD,
ROUNDED
QUARTERS.

RAFTER-
HIPPED
TYPE.

BOTH POINTS OF THE HIPS SHOULD
BE SIMILAR AND ON THE SAME
LEVEL. THE CROUP SHOULD BE
FAIRLY LEVEL WITH THE TAIL
ATTACHED HIGH FOR BEAUTY OF
OUTLINE. THE QUARTERS SHOULD
BE ROUND, WELL MUSCLED AND
STRONGLY JOIN THE GASKIN.
BECAUSE THE HINDQUARTERS
FURNISH THE POWER, MUSCLING
SHOULD BE SMOOTH AND WELL-
DEFINED.

The Hoof

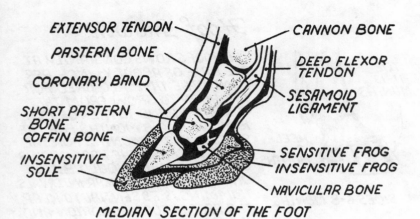

EXTENSOR TENDON
PASTERN BONE
CORONARY BAND
SHORT PASTERN BONE
COFFIN BONE
INSENSITIVE SOLE

CANNON BONE
DEEP FLEXOR TENDON
SESAMOID LIGAMENT
SENSITIVE FROG
INSENSITIVE FROG
NAVICULAR BONE

MEDIAN SECTION OF THE FOOT

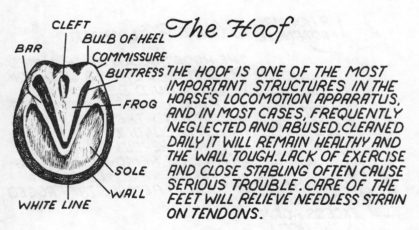

CLEFT
BULB OF HEEL
BAR
COMMISSURE
BUTTRESS
FROG
SOLE
WALL
WHITE LINE

The Hoof

THE HOOF IS ONE OF THE MOST IMPORTANT STRUCTURES IN THE HORSE'S LOCOMOTION APPARATUS, AND IN MOST CASES, FREQUENTLY NEGLECTED AND ABUSED. CLEANED DAILY IT WILL REMAIN HEALTHY AND THE WALL TOUGH. LACK OF EXERCISE AND CLOSE STABLING OFTEN CAUSE SERIOUS TROUBLE. CARE OF THE FEET WILL RELIEVE NEEDLESS STRAIN ON TENDONS.

19

Hoof Growth

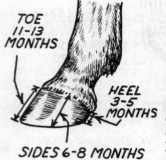

TOE
11-13
MONTHS

HEEL
3-5
MONTHS

SIDES 6-8 MONTHS

THE HOOF GROWS CONSTANTLY AT THE RATE OF ABOUT 1/3 INCH PER MONTH. THE TIME REQUIRED FOR THE HORN TO GROW FROM THE CORNARY BAND TO THE TOE IS 11-13 MONTHS, 6-8 MONTHS FOR THE SIDES AND 3-5 MONTHS FOR THE HEELS. BECAUSE THE HOOF GROWS CONSTANTLY IT SHOULD BE CUT OR TRIMMED AT REGULAR INTERVALS. TRIMMING IS ESSENTIAL TO KEEP THE FEET IN GOOD CONDITION AND IT ENCOURAGES EVEN GROWTH.

Hoof Trimming

A NORMAL FOOT ANGLE.

UNTRIMMED HOOF WITH EXCESS HORN AT THE TOE.

UNTRIMMED HOOF WITH EXCESS HORN ON THE HEEL.

THE HOOF SHOULD BE TRIMMED AT LEAST ONCE EVERY 8 WEEKS. THE WALLS SHOULD BE TRIMMED ONLY UNTIL THE FROG TOUCHES THE GROUND. THE SOLE SHOULD NEVER BE CUT, ONLY THOSE PARTS THAT WILL READILY FLAKE OFF SHOULD BE REMOVED. THE FROG SHOULD BE TRIMMED ONLY ENOUGH TO REMOVE THE RAGGED EDGES.

Shoes

BAR

THREE QUARTER

STRIP

TIP

THE BLACKSMITH POSSESSES AN INTIMATE KNOWLEDGE OF HORSE'S FEET AND IS AN EXPERT AT SHAPING SHOES TO FIT INDIVIDUAL CASES. THE BAR SHOE IS DESIGNED TO RAISE THE HEEL AND RELIEVE THE BACK TENDONS. THE THREE-QUARTER SHOE IS USED WHEN A HORSE HAS SUFFERED FROM CORNS. TIPS ARE USED FOR HORSES AT PASTURE IF THE GROUND IS HARD OR FEET BRITTLE. THE STRIP SHOE KEEPS A DRESSING IN PLACE.

Shoeing Damage

 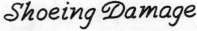

THE AREA WEAKENED BY NAILS.

WALL TORN AWAY AS A RESULT OF THE HORSE STEPPING ON SHOE AND PULLING IT OFF.

FOR DOMESTIC USE IT HAS BEEN FOUND NECESSARY, IN MOST CASES, TO PROTECT THE HORSE'S HOOFS WITH STEEL SHOES. ALTHOUGH THESE SHOES DO PROTECT AGAINST EXTENSIVE WEAR, THEY ALSO DAMAGE THE HOOF. EVERY NAIL DRIVEN INTO THE WALL DESTROYS THE TUBULAR HOOF FIBERS AND WEAKENS THE PART. WHERE CONDITIONS PERMIT, HOOFS LEFT UNSHOD WILL BE STRONGER AND HEALTHIER.

Unshod Hoofs

WHEN THE HORSE IS RIDDEN ON SOFT GROUND, SHOES ARE NOT NECESSARY AND THE ANIMAL IS REALLY BETTER OFF WITHOUT THEM. THE FEET OF A BAREFOOT HORSE WILL STAND MUCH MORE NEGLECT THAN THOSE OF A SHOD HORSE. BUT EVEN UNSHOD FEET SHOULD BE INSPECTED OFTEN TO DETECT ANY IRREGULARITIES OF THEIR GROWTH. UNSHOD FEET DO NOT NEED TRIMMING AS OFTEN AS THOSE WITH SHOES.

HORSES PASTURED FOR LONG PERIODS SHOULD GO BAREFOOT.

The Teeth

Teeth

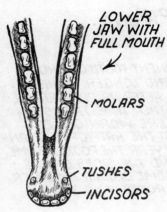

LOWER JAW WITH FULL MOUTH

MOLARS

TUSHES

INCISORS

BORN TOOTHLESS, A FOAL WILL CUT MILK TEETH IN 10 DAYS. THE LATERAL INCISORS ARE CUT IN 4-6 WEEKS AND THE THIRD PAIR IN 6-9 MONTHS. THE MILK TEETH ARE REPLACED BY PERMANENT INCISORS. AT 4 YEARS THE LATERAL AND FINALLY THE CORNER INCISORS AT 5 YEARS. WHEN THE HORSE REACHES 5 YEARS OF AGE HE HAS A FULL MOUTH. THE MATURE MALE HAS A TOTAL OF 40 TEETH, THE FEMALE ONLY 36.

Milk Teeth

PERMANENT TOOTH

CROWN

FANG

NECK

CROWN

MILK TOOTH

FANG

THE EXPERIENCED HORSEMAN SHOULD ALWAYS BE ABLE TO TELL THE DIFFERENCE BETWEEN MILK TEETH AND PERMANENT TEETH. MILK TEETH ARE SMALL, PURE WHITE IN COLOR AND SHOW A DISTINCT NECK AT THE GUM LINE. PERMANENT TEETH ARE MUCH LARGER, DARKER IN COLOR AND HAVE A BROADER NECK WHICH SHOWS NO CONSTRICTION AT THE GUM LINE.

Tooth Wear

WORN OFF

OLD ⟵ ⟶ YOUNG

THE CHART ABOVE
SHOWS THE NIPPERS
AS THEY ARE WORN
DOWN WITH AGE.

EACH PERMANENT TOOTH OF A HORSE
IS LARGER AND LONGER WITHIN A
SHORT TIME AFTER ITS APPEARANCE
THAN ANY OTHER TIME. THE TOOTH
SURFACES ARE WORN OFF BY
GRINDING AT THE RATE OF $\frac{1}{12}$ OF AN
INCH EVERY YEAR. THE ROOTS BECOME
SHORTER AND THE SIDES OF THE
JAWBONE COME CLOSER TOGETHER
BELOW THE ROOTS.

Changes

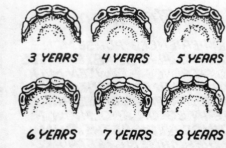

3 YEARS   4 YEARS   5 YEARS

6 YEARS   7 YEARS   8 YEARS

9 YEARS   15 YEARS   20 YEARS

THE INCISORS SHOW CHANGES
WITH AGE. AT 6 YEARS THE CUPS
ARE ALREADY DISAPPEARING
AND AT 9 THEY HAVE ALL GONE.
NOTE AT 9 YEARS HOW THE TEETH
SHOW SIGNS OF CHANGING SHAPE.
AT 15 YEARS ALL THE INCISORS
HAVE CHANGED SHAPE AND AT
20 THEY SHOW GREATER DEPTH
THAN WIDTH.

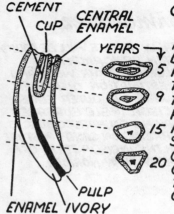

CEMENT
CUP
CENTRAL ENAMEL
YEARS
5
9
15
20
PULP
ENAMEL / IVORY

Tooth Structure

ILLUSTRATED ON THIS PAGE IS A DRAWING OF A HORSE'S LOWER PINCER TOOTH. IT CLEARLY ILLUSTRATES WHY, WITH ADVANCING AGE, THE TEETH SLANT OUT TOWARD THE FRONT, CHANGE IN WEARING SURFACE AS SHOWN IN CROSS SECTIONAL SHAPES, AND THE CHANGES IN THE CUPS AND THEIR DISAPPEARANCE. CUP CHANGES ENABLE HORSEMEN TO JUDGE THE AGE OF A HORSE WITH CLOSE ACCURACY UP TO 12 YEARS.

THE SEVEN-YEAR HOOK IS ALSO A MEANS OF ESTIMATING AGE.

GALVAYNE'S GROOVE

Age Estimation

ESTABLISHING THE AGE OF A HORSE THROUGH TOOTH APPEARANCE MEANS EXPERIENCE AND THE BEST WAY TO LEARN IS TO EXAMINE TEETH IN HORSES OF KNOWN AGES. GALVAYNE'S GROOVE, WHICH APPEARS AT THE GUM MARGIN IN 10 YEARS, EXTENDS HALF WAY DOWN THE TOOTH AT 15 AND REACHES THE TABLE MARGIN AT 20 YEARS, IS OFTEN USED BY HORSEMEN AS A MEANS OF AGE ESTIMATION.

27

Abnormalities

OCCASIONALLY HORSES WILL BE FOUND WITH CERTAIN ABNORMALITIES WHICH INFLUENCE TOOTH WEAR AND MAKE AGE ESTIMATION DIFFICULT. CRIBBERS WEAR THE OUTER EDGES OF THE INCISOR TABLE SURFACES FROM GNAWING ON HARD OBJECTS. HORSES GRAZING ON SANDY PASTURE WILL WEAR THE INCISOR TEETH OFF MORE RAPIDLY THAN NORMAL.

THE PARROT MOUTH, SHOWING AN OVERSHOT JAW, CAUSES UNEVEN WEAR OF THE LOWER INCISORS.

Dentistry

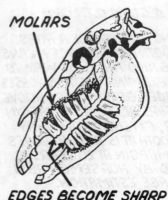

MOLARS

EDGES BECOME SHARP

THE AVERAGE HORSE'S TEETH KEEP SOUND AND DECAY IS UNCOMMON. BUT IRREGULAR GROWTH OF TOOTH EDGES, ESPECIALLY IN OLDER HORSES, OFTEN REQUIRES ATTENTION. THE MOLAR EDGES MAY BECOME SHARP ON THE OUTER EDGES AND CAUSE INJURY TO THE INSIDE OF THE CHEEKS. SHARP MOLARS CAN OFTEN BE DEALT WITH BY THE OWNER WITH A RASP. SERIOUS IRREGULARITIES WILL REQUIRE A VETERINARY.

INCISORS
OF A 7
YEAR OLD
HORSE.

Tampered Teeth

FOR THE PURPOSE OF DECEPTION,
UNSCRUPULOUS HORSEMEN EN-
DEAVOR TO MAKE THE AMATEUR A
VICTIM OF TRADE TRICKS BY ALTER-
ING THE NORMAL APPEARANCE OF
A HORSE'S TEETH. THIS TAMPERING
INVOLVES FILING, STAINING AND
EVEN DRILLING TO MAKE THE TEETH
LOOK LIKE THOSE OF A YOUNGER
ANIMAL. SUCH PRACTICE IS OFTEN
REFERRED TO AS BISHOPING.

INCISORS
OF A 20
YEAR OLD
HORSE.

Illness and Injury

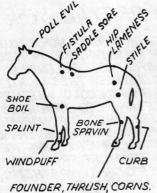

POLL EVIL
FISTULA
SADDLE SORE
HIP
LAMENESS
STIFLE
SHOE BOIL
SPLINT
BONE SPAVIN
WINDPUFF
CURB

FOUNDER, THRUSH, CORNS.

Unsoundness

UNLIKE OTHER DOMESTICATED ANIMALS, HORSES ARE UNUSUALLY SUSCEPTIBLE TO DISEASES OF A DISABLING NATURE. SOME ARE HEREDITARY. OTHERS ARE BY-PRODUCTS OF DOMESTICITY. FAILURE TO OBSERVE PROPER BALANCE OF WORK AND REST, IMPROPER SHOEING AND FAULTY CONDITIONING ALL CONTRIBUTE TO UNSOUNDNESS.

THE CHARACTERISTIC POSTURE OF A SICK HORSE.

Symptoms

THE MOST COMMON INDICATIONS OF DISEASE ARE PARTIAL OR COMPLETE LOSS OF APPETITE, ELEVATION OF TEMPERATURE, INCREASED PULSE, ACCELERATED BREATHING, LISTLESSNESS, STIFFNESS, NASAL DISCHARGE, COUGHING AND DIARRHEA. EVERY DISEASE HAS DIFFERENT INDICATIONS AND SYMPTOMS. THEY VARY SO THAT ONLY EXHAUSTIVE STUDY CAN ACQUAINT ONE WITH ALL OF THEM.

33

Care Of The Sick

FOR A SICK OR INJURED HORSE ALLOW PLENTY OF FRESH AIR, BUT PROTECT FROM DRAFTS. PROVIDE PLENTY OF BEDDING AND KEEP FRESH WATER WITHIN REACH. IN COLD WEATHER A BLANKET AND LEG BANDAGES MAY BE REQUIRED FOR WARMTH. A SICK HORSE SHOULD NEVER BE LEFT ALONE FOR VERY LONG, HE DERIVES COMFORT FROM THE PRESENCE OF A SYMPATHETIC, GENTLE ATTENDANT.

100°F

101.5°F

Temperature

NORMAL BODY TEMPERATURE OF THE HORSE AT REST IS 100°F, BUT MAY VARY ONE DEGREE EITHER WAY. IT VARIES WITH EXERCISE, EXCITEMENT AND AIR TEMPERATURES. HARD, FAST WORK, ESPECIALLY UNDER A HOT SUN, MAY BUILD THE BODY HEAT TO 104° TO 107°. AT THIS READING THE HORSE IS APPROACHING OVERHEATING. THE NEW FOAL HAS A TEMPERATURE OF 101.5°F, OVER 102° SHOULD BE LOOKED ON AS ABNORMAL.

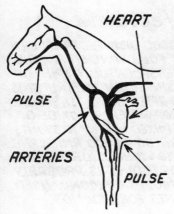

HEART

PULSE

ARTERIES

PULSE

Pulse

THE PULSE OF A HORSE MAY BE TAKEN FROM EITHER THE SUBMARILLARY ARTERY WHICH PASSES UNDER THE JAW ON EITHER SIDE OR FROM THE RADIAL ARTERY LOCATED INSIDE THE FORELEGS ON A LEVEL WITH THE ANIMAL'S ELBOW. THE NORMAL PULSE RATE OF A HORSE IS 36 TO 40 BEATS PER MINUTE. THE PULSE IS THE EXPANSION AND CONTRACTION OF THE ARTERIES.

LEG BANDAGES
GAUZE PADS
STERILE COTTON
VASELINE
BORIC ACID
EPSOM SALTS
IODINE
METHYLENE BLUE
LINAMENT
SULFA POWDER
HYDROGEN PEROXIDE
SCARLET OIL
ALCOHOL
BLOOD STOPPER
THERMOMETER
SCISSORS
SHARP KNIFE
TWEEZERS

Medical Kit

EVERYONE WHO OWNS A HORSE SHOULD ALWAYS HAVE FIRST AID SUPPLIES ON HAND AND KNOW HOW TO USE THEM. THE NECESSARY SUPPLIES ARE NOT EXPENSIVE AND MANY CAN BE FOUND AT THE LOCAL DRUG STORE. LISTED ON THIS PAGE ARE SUGGESTED SUPPLIES FOR THE HORSEMAN'S MEDICAL KIT.

BALLING GUN
20 cc HYPODERMIC
SYRINGE
WATER PAIL

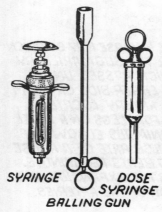

SYRINGE

DOSE
SYRINGE

BALLING GUN

Disinfectants

LYSOL IS A GOOD DISINFECTANT WHEN USED AT THE FOLLOWING STRENGTHS: WOUNDS: I TEASPOONFUL TO I PINT OF WATER. TO DISINFECTANT INSTRUMENTS BEFORE AND AFTER USE: 2 TEASPOONSFUL TO I PINT OF WATER. PEROXIDE OF HYDROGEN MIXED $\frac{1}{2}$ PINT TO 5 PINTS OF WATER IS ALSO A GOOD ANTISEPTIC FOR CLEANING WOUNDS. ORDINARY TINCTURE OF IODINE IS **PROBABLY** ONE OF THE MOST COMMONLY USED DISINFECTANTS FOR WOUNDS.

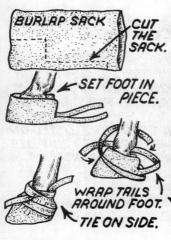

BURLAP SACK

CUT THE SACK.

SET FOOT IN PIECE.

WRAP TAILS AROUND FOOT.

TIE ON SIDE.

Poultice

AN EFFECTIVE, YET SIMPLE POULTICE CAN BE MADE BY MIXING BRAN WITH BOILING WATER. TO MAKE THE MIXTURE ANTISEPTIC SIMPLY ADD A HANDFUL OF SALT TO EACH HALF BUCKET OF BRAN. IF THE CONTINUED USE OF A POULTICE IS FOUND NECESSARY, GRADUALLY REDUCE THE QUANTITY OF SALT AFTER THE FIRST APPLICATION. TYPE OF BANDAGE FOR APPLYING A POULTICE TO THE FOOT.

Leg Bandage

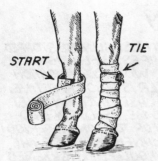

START

TIE

FOR THE INEXPERIENCED THE MOST ADAPTABLE BANDAGE TO USE IS A NONELASTIC COTTON SURGICAL TYPE 3 OR 4 INCHES WIDE. THE BANDAGE SHOULD BE DRY WHEN APPLIED AS A WET ONE WILL SHRINK AND PRODUCE SWELLING AND SORENESS. NEVER START AT THE FRONT OF LEG, BACK OVER THE TENDONS OR A WOUND.

TIE OFF BANDAGE ON OUTSIDE OF LEG.

Cold Water

GARDEN HOSE.

TIE HOSE TO LEG.

COTTON

FLANNEL BANDAGE.

WHEN THERE IS A NEED FOR COLD WATER BANDAGES, A FLANNEL SHOULD ALWAYS BE USED. THESE SHOULD BE KEPT WET AT ALL TIMES OR THEY WILL ACT AS HOT WATER BANDAGES. COMMON SODA ADDED TO THE WATER, IN WHICH THE BANDAGES ARE STEEPED, WILL HAVE THE EFFECT OF MAKING THE WATER COOLER.

A GARDEN HOSE INSERTED INTO TOP OF BANDAGE WITH TAP TURNED ON SLOWLY WILL KEEP BANDAGES COLD AND WET.

Bleeding

THE TOURNIQUET SHOULD BE USED WITH EXTREME CAUTION.

BLEEDING CAN USUALLY BE STOPPED WITH A COMPRESS HELD TIGHTLY AGAINST THE WOUND. APPLICATION OF COLD WATER IS ALSO EFFECTIVE. IN EXTREME CASES A TOURNIQUET MAY HAVE TO BE USED. APPLIED TOO TIGHTLY FOR TOO LONG A PERIOD IT CAN DO PERMANENT DAMAGE. THE TOURNIQUET SHOULD BE TIGHTENED SLOWLY UNTIL THE FLOW OF BLOOD STOPS. RELEASE EVERY 20 MINUTES. AFTER A MINUTE TIGHTEN AGAIN.

Colic

COLIC WILL OFTEN CAUSE VIOLENT ROLLING.

WHEN A HORSE SUDDENLY BECOMES UNEASY, PAWS AND KEEPS LOOKING AT HIS FLANKS, COLIC IS SUSPECTED. BROUGHT ON BY OVER-EATING, SPOILED FEEDS AND EATING WHILE FATIGUED, COLIC IS THE MOST COMMON CAUSE OF DEATH AMONG HORSES. FOR THE COLICKY HORSE APPLY HOT BLANKETS AROUND BELLY AND FLANKS TO REDUCE PAIN AND STIMULATE THE BOWEL ACTION. A VETERINARY SHOULD BE CALLED.

38

Heaves

THE SHAPE OF A HORSE WITH HEAVES CHANGES; THE ANIMAL WILL DEVELOP A LARGE STOMACH AND THE FLANKS WILL FALL AWAY.

WHEN A HORSE IS AFFECTED WITH HEAVES HE HAS DIFFICULTY IN FORCING AIR OUT OF HIS LUNGS. THIS CAUSES A CHARACTERISTIC MOVEMENT IN THE FLANKS. CAUSED BY DUSTY FEEDS OR LONG CONFINEMENT IN POORLY VENTILATED STABLES, HEAVES ARE ALSO OFTEN CHARACTERIZED BY A FREQUENT DRY COUGH. THE CONDITION CAN BE HELPED, BUT IT IS NOT CURABLE.

Tetanus

A SERIOUS DISEASE CAUSED BY GERMS WHICH ENTER THE SYSTEM THROUGH A DEEP PUNCTURE TYPE WOUND. THE EARLY SYMPTOMS ARE A GENERAL STIFFENING OF THE LIMBS AND MUSCLES OF THE JAWS. THE DEATH RATE FROM TETANUS IS HIGH AND INJECTIONS OF ANTI-TETANUS ARE GREATLY RECOMMENDED FOR ALL DEEP WOUNDS.

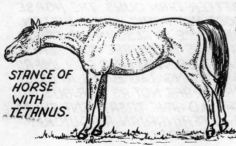

STANCE OF HORSE WITH TETANUS.

39

Sunstroke

SUNSTROKE IS USUALLY CAUSED FROM OVERWORKING A HORSE IN HOT WEATHER. SYMPTOMS ARE STAGGERING, THE NASAL MEMBRANES TURN A BLUISH-RED AND THE BODY MUSCLES TREMBLE. APPLY LARGE AMOUNTS OF WATER TO THE ANIMAL'S ENTIRE BODY. THEN RUB THE LEGS AND BODY VIGOROUSLY. ALLOW THE ANIMAL 2 DAYS OF COMPLETE REST.

APPLY COLD WATER TO THE ANIMAL'S HEAD WITH A LARGE SPONGE.

Snake Bite

THE CHANCE OF THE HORSE WITH SNAKE BITE IS REALLY MUCH BETTER THAN OURS. THE HORSE DOES NOT PANIC WHEN BITTEN AND SIZE IS ALSO IN HIS FAVOR. MUZZLE BITES ARE VERY SERIOUS BECAUSE SWELLING CAN IMPAIR BREATHING. LEG BITES, IN MOST CASES, ARE NOT AS SERIOUS, BUT SHOULD HAVE TREATMENT FROM A VETERINARIAN AS QUICKLY AS POSSIBLE.

Snake Bite First Aid

APPLY A LITTLE VASELINE TO THE HOSE BEFORE INSERTING INTO NOSTRIL.

RUBBER OR PLASTIC HOSE.

TAPE HOSE TO THE MUZZLE TO PREVENT IT'S SLIPPING OUT.

IN CASE OF A SNAKE BITE ON THE LEG APPLY A TOURNIQUET ABOVE BITE AND KEEP THE HORSE QUIET. ICE PACKS WILL HELP SLOW THE SPREAD OF VENOM AND REDUCE SWELLING UNTIL THE VETERINARIAN ARRIVES. IN EXTREME CASES OF MUZZLE BITES IT MAY BE NECESSARY TO INSERT A PIECE OF HOSE INTO THE SWOLLEN NOSTRIL TO PERMIT THE HORSE TO BREATHE.

Snake Bite Symptoms

FANGS

A BITE

BLOOD SPOTS →

TWO PIN PRICKS IN THE SKIN ARE EVIDENCE OF SNAKE BITE, BUT ARE NOT EASILY FOUND ON HORSES BECAUSE OF THE HAIR. SPOTS OF BLOOD WILL OFTEN INDICATE LOCATION.

IF THE SNAKE BITE HAS HAPPENED A CONSIDERABLE TIME BEFORE DISCOVERY THE SYMPTOMS ARE OFTEN ALARMING. THE HORSE MAY STAND SPRADDLE-LEGGED IN THE FRONT AND A BLOOD STAINED FROTH MAY HANG FROM BOTH NOSTRILS. BREATHING MAY BE LABORED AND THE EYELIDS AND NOSTRILS WILL BE SWOLLEN.

41

←FLOWERS, WHITE OR CREAM TO PURPLE IN COLOR.

WILD PLANTS, SUCH AS LOCOWEED, OFTEN FOUND GROWING IN PASTURES, ARE VERY POISONOUS TO HORSES.

Lead Poisoning

BECAUSE MANY HORSES LIKE THE TASTE OF PAINT IT IS BEST TO USE ONLY LEAD-FREE PAINTS FOR THE STABLE AND FENCES. SYMPTOMS OF LEAD POISONING, OFTEN CAUSED BY THE HORSE EATING PAINTED WOOD ARE CHOKING, SLOBBERING, COLIC AND LOSS OF APPETITE. CALL A VETERINARY AT ONCE. SPEED IS AN IMPORTANT FACTOR IN SAVING A POISONED ANIMAL.

WARBLES ARE OFTEN FOUND ON THE MUZZLE BUT MAY APPEAR AT ANY LOCATION ON THE HORSE.

WARBLES

Warbles

HARD LUMPS FOUND ON THE HORSE IN THE SPRING AND EARLY SUMMER ARE OFTEN WARBLES. THEY ARE NOT INFECTIOUS AS THEY ARE CAUSED FROM THE MAGGOT OF THE WARBLE FLY. WHEN RIPE A SMALL HOLE APPEARS IN THE CENTER OF THE LUMP THROUGH WHICH THE MAGGOT WILL EMERGE. A POULTICE APPLIED TO THE LUMP WILL HASTEN IT TO RIPEN.

Poll Evil

POLL EVIL IS SLOW TO YIELD TO TREATMENT AND MAY BREAK OUT AGAIN AFTER IT HAS BEEN CURED.

CAUSED BY A BLOW ON THE TOP OF THE HEAD, POLL EVIL IS INDICATED BY A SOFT SWELLING BETWEEN THE EARS. THE REGION IS HOT AND THE PRESSURE OF PUS MAY PRODUCE A STIFF NECK. COLD PACKS SHOULD BE APPLIED AND VETERINARY AID CALLED IN. SURGICAL TREATMENT AND THE ADMINISTRATION OF ANTIBIOTICS ARE USUALLY REQUIRED.

Eye Care

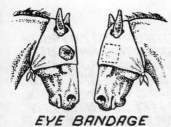

EYE BANDAGE

OPENINGS STERILE PAD. FOR EARS AND EYE.

A WATERY EYE OR FLOW OF TEARS IS USUALLY A SYMPTOM OF A FOREIGN OBJECT IN THE EYE. FLOOD THE EYE WITH CLEAN WATER. THEN FLOOD IT WITH BORIC ACID SOLUTION WHICH IS PREPARED BY DISSOLVING 2 SPOONFULS IN 1 CUP OF WARM WATER. IF THE OBJECT HAS CAUSED ANY INJURY TO THE EYEBALL, CALL IN A VETERINARY.

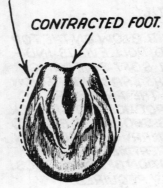

SHAPE OF NORMAL FOOT.

CONTRACTED FOOT.

Contracted Heels

CAUSED BY NEGLECTED SHOEING AND EXTREME DRYNESS OF THE HOOF, CONTRACTION IS GENERALLY FOUND IN THE FOREFEET AND MAY CAUSE INTERMITTENT LAMENESS. THE FOOT LOSES ITS CIRCULAR SHAPE AS THE HEELS BEND TOWARDS EACH OTHER AND SQUEEZE THE BRANCHES OF THE FROG BETWEEN THEM. THE TREATMENT INVOLVES SPECIAL SHOEING AND SOAKING.

GROUND SURFACE OF THE HOOF SHOWING LOCATION OF CORNS.

Corns

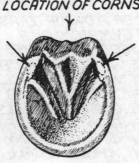

CORNS ARE OFTEN CAUSED BY FAULTY SHOEING OR SHOES THAT HAVE BEEN LEFT ON TOO LONG. CORNS, WHICH ARE A BRUISE OF THE SENSITIVE SOLE, USUALLY APPEAR ON THE INNER SIDE OF THE FRONT FEET. LAMENESS MAY SUDDENLY APPEAR WHILE THE HORSE IS AT WORK; AFTER A FEW DAY'S TRAVEL THE HORSE MAY APPEAR SOUND, BUT THE LAMENESS MAY SUDDENLY REAPPEAR. THE SHOE SHOULD BE REMOVED, THE CORN PARED OUT TO RELIEVE PRESSURE AND ANTISEPTIC SHOULD THEN BE APPLIED.

44

Dry Hoof

CHIPPING AND CRACKS
ARE SIGNS OF DRYNESS.

DURING THE SUMMER THE HOOF MAY BECOME HARD AND BRITTLE THROUGH LACK OF MOISTURE. THIS CONDITION RETARDS HOOF GROWTH AND IT BECOMES MORE SUSCEPTIBLE TO DISEASE AND INJURY. DRYNESS MAY BE CORRECTED BY STANDING THE HORSE IN WATER OR ATTACH WET BURLAP PIECES OVER HOOFS AND KEEP WET. MOISTURE CAN BE RETAINED BY APPLYING A PURE LINSEED OIL.

Founder

AS FOUNDER PROGRESSES THE FOOT UNDERGOES STRUCTURAL CHANGES. RINGS APPEAR AND THE HOOF BECOMES DEFORMED THROUGH A BULGING SOLE.

BECAUSE THE HOOF AND SOLE DO NOT ALLOW MUCH EXPANSION, THE ABNORMAL INCREASE IN THE BLOOD CIRCULATION TO THE FOOT CAUSED BY FOUNDER MEANS GREAT PAIN AND PRESSURE. CAUSED BY EATING OR DRINKING WHILE HOT OR STANDING IDLE. FOUNDERED HORSES BECOME SUSCEPTIBLE TO REPEATED ATTACKS WHICH MAY CAUSE TOTAL FOOT DAMAGE. REMOVE THE SHOE AND PLACE FOOT ALTERNATELY IN HOT AND COLD WATER.

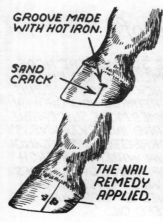

GROOVE MADE
WITH HOT IRON.

SAND
CRACK

THE NAIL
REMEDY
APPLIED.

Sand Crack

A CRACK IN THE WALL OF THE HOOF
RUNNING DOWNWARDS FROM THE
CORONET IS CONSIDERED A SAND
CRACK. DRY, BRITTLE HOOFS, OFTEN
CAUSED BY RASPING AWAY THE OUT-
SIDE WALL, WILL CAUSE THE CRACK.
LAMENESS DOES NOT ALWAYS APPEAR
AND SAND CRACK IS RARELY FOUND
IN THE HIND HOOFS. THE CRACK MAY
BE ISOLATED BY MAKING A GROOVE
WITH A HOT IRON. SOMETIMES A SHOE-
ING NAIL DRIVEN THROUGH THE WALL
AND CLINCHED OVER IS USED.

NAVICULAR
BONE.

SYMPTOMS OF NAVICULAR
DISEASE ARE: POINTING
OUT OF THE FOOT, HEAT
IN THE FOOT, LAMENESS
WHICH MAY WEAR OFF
WITH EXERCISE.

Navicular Disease

ONE OF THE MOST SERIOUS DISEASES
THAT A HORSE CAN HAVE, NAVICULAR
IS A CORROSIVE ULCER ON THE
NAVICULAR BONE. USUALLY FOUND
IN THE FOREFEET, THE CONDITION
IS OFTEN CAUSED BY CONTINUED
USE ON HARD ROADS. ALTHOUGH
PROGRESS OF NAVICULAR DISEASE
IS QUITE SLOW, SOONER OR LATER
THE ANIMAL'S USEFULNESS WILL
COME TO AN END.

LOCATION OF SCRATCHES ON THE HEEL.

Scratches

EARLY INDICATION OF SCRATCHES IS A SWELLING OF THE BULBS OF THE HEELS. THE SKIN BECOMES HOT AND AS THE SWELLING INCREASES, CRACKS APPEAR. THEN A FLUID POURS OUT OF THESE CRACKS AND AS IT DRIES, THE CRACKS GROW DEEPER AND LONGER. A COLD, MILD DISINFECTANT AND GAUZE BANDAGE SHOULD BE APPLIED.

TIE IN FRONT

GAUZE PAD

GAUZE BANDAGE

MEDIAN CLEFT OF THE FROG.

Thrush

A DISEASE OF THE FEET CAUSED BY FAILURE TO OBSERVE PROPER SANITARY CONDITIONS IN THE STALL. INVOLVING PRINCIPALLY THE FROG, THRUSH IS CHARACTER-IZED BY THE DISCHARGE OF DARK FOUL SMELLING MATTER FROM THE CLEFTS OF THE FROG. THE TREATMENT IS A GERMICIDAL DRESSING HELD IN PLACE BY A SHOEING PAD.

LATERAL CLEFT OF THE FROG.

47

Quittor

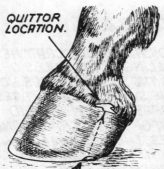

QUITTOR LOCATION.

ARROW ILLUSTRATES PUS WORKING UPWARD FROM CORN.

A RUNNING SORE SITUATED ON OR JUST ABOVE THE CORONET, OFTEN CAUSED FROM A BLOW, QUITTOR MAY ALSO ARISE FROM A NAIL PUNCTURE IN THE SOLE OF THE FOOT OR A SUPPURATING CORN. SWELLING APPEARS ABOVE THE CORONET AND MAY SPREAD UP THE CANNON. THE HORSE MAY REFUSE TO PLACE WEIGHT ON THE FOOT. THE CONDITION OFTEN REQUIRES SURGICAL ATTENTION TO PERMIT FREE DRAINAGE.

Side Bone

A HARD LUMP AND HEAT ON THE CORONET ON EITHER SIDE OF THE HEEL INDICATES SIDE BONE.

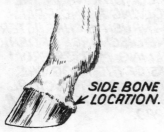

SIDE BONE LOCATION.

A BONY GROWTH ON EITHER LATERAL CARTILAGE OF THE FOOT, SIDE BONE IS OFTEN CAUSED BY FAST GAITS ON HARD ROADS. PROGRESS OF THE CONDITION IS SLOW AND IF THE HORSE IS NOT LAME, SOAK THE FOOT FOR 2 DAYS AND THEN APPLY HOOF DRESSING TO AID THE HOOF IN RETAINING MOISTURE. PERSISTENT LAMENESS WILL REQUIRE SPECIAL SHOEING.

48

REST AND SPECIAL
SHOEING WILL HELP
THE CONDITION.

Ringbone

AN ENLARGEMENT APPEARING ON
THE PASTERN BONES BETWEEN
THE UPPER EDGE OF THE HOOF AND
THE LOWER EDGE OF THE FETLOCK
JOINT. CAUSED BY A BLOW OR
THE SHOE BEING LEFT ON TOO
LONG, RINGBONE'S GROWTH IS
GRADUAL AND LAMENESS MAY
BE PRESENT WEEKS BEFORE
ANY ENLARGEMENT IS NOTICED.
RINGBONE IS GENERALLY NOT
CURABLE.

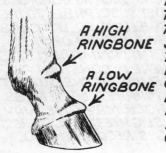

A HIGH
RINGBONE

A LOW
RINGBONE

Capped Hock

CAPPED
HOCK

LEATHER
HOCK
BOOT

KICKING IN THE STALL OR A SHORTAGE
OF BEDDING ARE MAJOR CAUSES OF
CAPPED HOCK. A SWELLING OCCURS
ON THE UPPER POINT OF THE HOCK
BONE AND IT IS HOT AND PAINFUL.
LAMENESS MAY OR MAY NOT BE
PRESENT. TREATMENT INVOLVES THE
REMOVAL OF THE CAUSE OF INJURY.
SUFFICIENT BEDDING OR A LEATHER
HOCK BOOT WILL PROTECT AGAINST
THE CONDITION RE-OCCURING.

Curb

HORSES WITH SICKLE HOCKS ARE MORE LIABLE TO CURBS THAN ANY OTHERS.

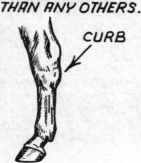

CURB

HORSES THAT PUT HEAVY STRAIN ON THE HOCKS, SUCH AS JUMPERS, ARE THE MOST SUSCEPTIBLE TO THE PAINFUL SWELLING CALLED CURB. CAUSED BY A STRAIN OF THE LIGAMENT, INFLAMMATION SETS IN AND THERE IS CONSTANT FILLING IN OF FLUID. AT THE OUTSET THERE IS MARKED LAMENESS AND THE HOCK MAY GIVE WAY WITH THE SLIGHTEST EFFORT. REST AND FIRING IS RECOMMENDED.

Bog Spavin

SPECIAL SHOEING WILL OFTEN RETARD THE PROGRESS OF BOG SPAVIN.

BOG SPAVIN IS A ROUND, SMOOTH, WELL DEFINED FLUCTUATING BUNCH.

CAUSED BY SOME STRAIN, SUCH AS SLIPPING, BOG SPAVIN IS A CHRONIC, PUFFY, SWELLING ON THE INSIDE AND A LITTLE TO THE FRONT OF THE HOCK. IN MOST CASES LAMENESS IS ABSENT AND A BLISTER APPLIED EVERY SIX WEEKS WILL CAUSE THE SWELLING TO GROW SMALLER AND FINALLY DISAPPEAR. THE PRESENCE OF BOG SPAVIN FREQUENTLY INDICATES INHERENT WEAKNESS.

50

A CONFIRMED BONE SPAVIN CAN END THE USEFULNESS AND VALUE OF A HORSE.

Bone Spavin

A BONY GROWTH THROWN OUT ON THE INNER AND LOWER PART OF THE HOCK, BONE SPAVIN IS OFTEN CAUSED BY UNDUE CONCUSSION OR STRAIN. IN THE EARLY STAGES ONE MAY NOT BE ABLE TO DETECT ANY ENLARGEMENT, YET THE HORSE IS LAME AND HE CANNOT BEND HIS HOCK PROPERLY. THE TREATMENT IS USUALLY REST AND BLISTERING, BUT MANY OF THE CASES ARE INCURABLE.

Lymphangitis

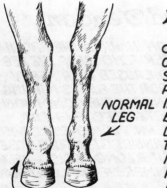

NORMAL LEG

LEG WITH LYMPHANGITIS.

OVER FEEDING AN IDLE HORSE WILL OFTEN BRING ON LYMPHANGITIS. THE SYMPTOMS ARE THE SUDDEN AP-PEARANCE OF A SWELLING ON THE INSIDE OF THE THIGH ON ONE OR BOTH LEGS. THE SWELLING CONTINUES UNTIL THE ENTIRE LEG BECOMES ALMOST TWICE ITS SIZE. A HIGH BODY FEVER IS PRESENT AND THE BOWEL AND KIDNEY ACTIONS DECREASE. THE ATTENTION OF A VETERINARIAN IS USUALLY REQUIRED.

51

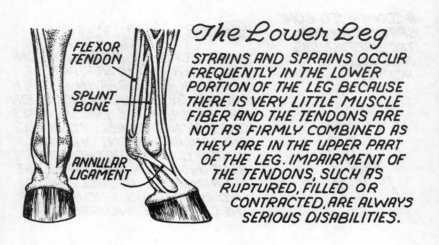

FLEXOR TENDON

SPLINT BONE

ANNULAR LIGAMENT

The Lower Leg

STRAINS AND SPRAINS OCCUR FREQUENTLY IN THE LOWER PORTION OF THE LEG BECAUSE THERE IS VERY LITTLE MUSCLE FIBER AND THE TENDONS ARE NOT AS FIRMLY COMBINED AS THEY ARE IN THE UPPER PART OF THE LEG. IMPAIRMENT OF THE TENDONS, SUCH AS RUPTURED, FILLED OR CONTRACTED, ARE ALWAYS SERIOUS DISABILITIES.

Bowed Tendon

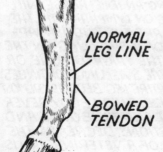

NORMAL LEG LINE

BOWED TENDON

A CONDITION IN WHICH THE PROFILE OF THE BACK TENDON OF THE LEG IS BULGED. CAUSED BY A HEAVY STRAIN UPON THE FIBERS MAKING UP THE TENDON, THE CONDITION IS CHARACTERIZED BY HEAT, SWELLING AND LAMENESS. BOWED TENDON CANNOT GENERALLY BE CURED, BUT A LONG PERIOD OF REST WILL IMPROVE THE CONDITION.

ALTHOUGH SMALL AT FIRST, IT IS COMMON FOR THEM TO BECOME QUITE LARGE.

Windgalls

CAUSED BY STRAIN AND HARD WORK, WINDGALLS WILL NOT NORMALLY CAUSE LAMENESS AND ARE NOT CONSIDERED A TECHNICAL UNSOUNDNESS. THE SMALL SACKS, FOUND ON BOTH FRONT AND BACK LEGS, ARE FIRM WHEN THE WEIGHT IS PLACED UPON THE FOOT AND SOFT WHEN THE FOOT IS PICKED UP. BY RAISING THE HEELS WITH SPECIAL SHOES THE STRAIN MAY BE ALLEVIATED.

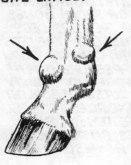

CAPPED ELBOW

Capped Elbow

A STUFFED LEATHER RING WORN AROUND THE CORONET WILL HELP PREVENT RECURRENCE OF A CAPPED ELBOW.

CAUSED BY BEING BRUISED FROM THE HEEL WHEN LYING DOWN OR FROM A LACK OF BEDDING, A CAPPED ELBOW IS A HEAVY TUMOR-LIKE GROWTH AND VARIES IN SIZE FROM 2 TO 10 INCHES IN DIAMETER. IT IS A BLEMISH, BUT RARELY CAUSES LAMENESS, EXCEPT PERHAPS DURING THE EARLY STAGES OF FORMATION.

Splint

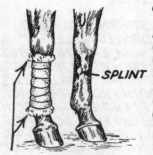

EXTEND COTTON BEYOND BANDAGES.

A SPLINT IS A BONY ENLARGEMENT ON THE CANNON OR SPLINT BONES, ON THE INSIDE OF THE FORE LEGS. SPLINTS ARE CAUSED BY THE LEGS BEING JARRED, BAD CONFORMATION OF THE FEET OR PRESSURE ON THE OUTSIDE OF THE FOOT FROM FAULTY SHOEING. AT THE OUTSET OF A SPLINT, COLD-WATER BANDAGES PROBABLY ARE THE BEST TREATMENT, BUT IN PERSISTENT CASES, BLISTERING OR PINFIRING MUST BE RESORTED TO.

Roundworms

THE ROUNDWORM IS WHITE IN COLOR AND GENERALLY AS THICK AS A PENCIL.

THE COMMONEST OF ALL WORMS FOUND IN THE HORSE IS THE ROUNDWORM. THEY VARY FROM 6 TO 22 INCHES IN LENGTH AND ARE FOUND IN THE SMALL IN-TESTINES. SMALL NUMBERS RARELY CAUSE ANY SYMPTOMS, BUT LARGE NUMBERS OF ROUNDWORMS CAUSE IRREGU-LARITY OF THE BOWELS, LOSS OF CONDITION AND INTERMITTENT COLIC.

54

BOTS
IN THE
STOMACH.

THE ADULT
BOT FLY.

Bots

THE STOMACH BOTS ARE NOT TRUE WORMS, BUT ARISE FROM THE BOT FLY WHICH LAYS ITS EGGS ON THE HORSE'S LEGS. WHEN THE HORSE BITES OR LICKS HIS LEGS THE EGGS ARE TRANSFERRED TO THE MOUTH AND THEN ON TO THE STOMACH WHERE THEY HATCH. LARGE QUANTITIES OF THESE BOTS CAUSE LOSS OF CONDITION AND A DULL, DRY COAT.

BOT EGGS.

SAND-
PAPER.

A PIECE OF MEDIUM GRIT SANDPAPER RUBBED WITH THE LAY OF THE HAIR WILL REMOVE EGGS.

Bot Eggs

THE BOT FLY APPEARS IN AUGUST AND HER TINY YELLOW EGGS WILL BE SEEN UPON THE HAIRS OF THE HORSE'S LEGS. THE EGGS SHOULD BE REMOVED BY CAREFULLY SCRAPING THE HAIR WITH A RAZOR BLADE OR RUB THE LEGS LIGHTLY WITH A KEROSENE CLOTH. IF THE EGGS ARE SCRAPED OFF THEY SHOULD BE CAUGHT IN A CONTAINER AND BURNED.

General Care

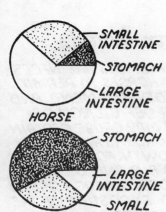

SMALL INTESTINE

STOMACH

LARGE INTESTINE

HORSE

STOMACH

LARGE INTESTINE

SMALL INTESTINE

COW

The Stomach

THE SIZE OF A HORSE'S STOMACH MAKES IT IMPERATIVE THAT FOOD BE GIVEN IN SMALL AMOUNTS AND AT FREQUENT INTERVALS. THE MAXIMUM CAPACITY IS ABOUT 4 GALLONS, BUT IT FUNCTIONS MOST EFFICIENTLY WITH NOT OVER 2½ GALLONS. THE DIAGRAM SHOWS A COMPARATIVE CAPACITY OF DIGESTIVE TRACTS BETWEEN THE HORSE AND COW.

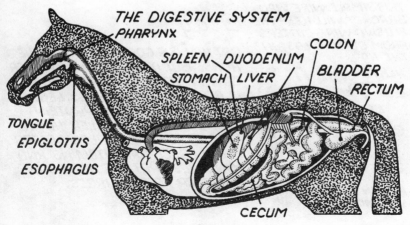

THE DIGESTIVE SYSTEM

PHARYNX

SPLEEN   DUODENUM   COLON

STOMACH   LIVER   BLADDER

RECTUM

TONGUE

EPIGLOTTIS

ESOPHAGUS

CECUM

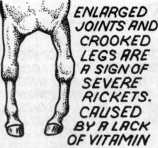

ENLARGED JOINTS AND CROOKED LEGS ARE A SIGN OF SEVERE RICKETS. CAUSED BY A LACK OF VITAMIN D OR CALCIUM, IT IS MOST COMMONLY FOUND IN FOALS.

Vitamin Needs

CERTAIN VITAMINS ARE NECESSARY FOR HORSES TO PERMIT GROWTH, DEVELOPMENT AND HEALTH. A DEFICIENCY OF VITAMIN A MAY CAUSE CERTAIN BONE DISORDERS AND POOR HOOF GROWTH. FORTUNATELY VITAMINS A, B AND D MAY ALL BE PROVIDED THROUGH GREEN HAYS AND EXPOSURE OF THE BODY TO DIRECT SUNLIGHT.

THIS SIMPLE WIRE WALL BRACKET WILL KEEP THE ELUSIVE WIRE CUTTERS FROM GETTING LOST IN THE HAY.

HEAVY WIRE

BEND

FASTEN TO WALL WITH SCREWS.

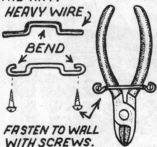

Hay

OAT HAY IS A GOOD FEED FOR THE HORSE, BUT IT HAS ONLY 7 TO 8 PER CENT PROTEIN COMPARED TO 11 TO 12 PER CENT FOR A GRASS LEGUME HAY. THE QUALITY OF PROTEIN FOUND IN GOOD ALFALFA HAY IS SECOND TO NONE. IT ALSO OFFERS MANY ESSENTIAL VITAMINS AND MINERALS THAT ARE NOT FOUND IN OTHER FEED SOURCES.

60

SCREW EYE

BOLT SNAP

GALVANIZED TUB MAKES GOOD GRAIN BUCKET.

Oats

OATS ARE THE SAFEST OF ALL GRAINS FOR THE HORSE BECAUSE THE ADHERENT HULLS AFFORD ENOUGH BULK TO PREVENT ERRORS IN FEEDING THAT ARE COMMON IN CONCENTRATED GRAINS. ABOUT 7 PER CENT OF DRY BRAN MIXED WITH THE OAT RATION WILL HELP PREVENT THE GREEDY EATER FROM BOLTING HIS OATS AND CHOKING HIMSELF. ROLLED OATS ARE CONSIDERED BETTER, BY MANY HORSEMEN, THAN WHOLE OATS.

GRAIN SCOOP

CUT PIECES FROM 1" THICK PINE.

WOOD SCREWS.

NAIL TIN TO WOOD.

HEAVY TIN.

CUT

Feeding Bran

UP TO 2 POUNDS OF DRY BRAN IS COMMONLY MIXED WITH THE GRAIN RATION. AN OCCASIONAL FEEDING OF A BRAN MASH IS RELISHED BY MOST HORSES AND IN THIS FORM BRAN HAS A PRONOUNCED LAXATIVE ACTION. USE ABOUT 2 TO 4 POUNDS OF BRAN, ONE SPOONFUL OF SALT AND MIX WITH BOILING WATER. COVER AND FEED WHEN COOL.

MAKE THIS HANDY SCOOP.

61

← PLASTIC TAPE

HACKSAW BLADE

AN OLD HACKSAW BLADE IS USEFUL IN SPRING TIME GROOMING. PULLED OVER THE HORSE'S BODY IT WILL REMOVE THE LOOSE WINTER HAIR.

Linseed Meal

AN EXCELLENT FEED SUPPLEMENT FOR HORSES THAT ARE IN A RUN-DOWN CONDITION, LINSEED MEAL ALSO HAS A SLIGHT LAXATIVE ACTION AND IT IMPROVES THE GLOSS OF THE COAT. ALTHOUGH IT IS USEFUL DURING SPRING SHEDDING, LINSEED MEAL IS NEVER FED IN LARGE AMOUNTS. A SPOONFUL MIXED WITH THE GRAIN RATION IS SUFFICIENT.

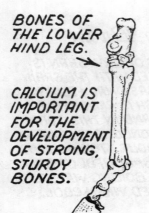

BONES OF THE LOWER HIND LEG. →

CALCIUM IS IMPORTANT FOR THE DEVELOPMENT OF STRONG, STURDY BONES.

Molasses

ALTHOUGH ITS NUTRITIVE VALUE IS SOMEWHAT LESS THAN THAT OF OATS, MOLASSES IS RELISHED BY HORSES AND THUS IS OFTEN VALUABLE AS AN APPETIZER. IF DILUTED WITH WATER, IT CAN BE SPRINKLED OVER HAY OR MIXED UNDILUTED WITH THE GRAIN. MOLASSES, ALSO A RICH SOURCE OF CALCIUM, HAS BEEN FED TO HORSES FOR YEARS WITH GOOD RESULTS.

Alfalfa Pellets

DEHYDRATED ALFALFA PELLETS PROVIDE A SOURCE OF PROTEIN FOR HORSES. THE LITTLE GREEN PELLETS CONTAIN THE SAME AMINO ACIDS FOUND IN LINSEED MEAL AND CONTAIN MANY NUTRITIONAL PROPERTIES NOT FOUND IN OTHER PROTEINS. DEHYDRATED ALFALFA PELLETS THAT CONTAIN THE PRESERVATIVE SANTOQUIN WILL KEEP THEIR VITAMIN CONTENT STABLE.

PROTEIN IS OF SPECIAL IMPORTANCE FOR THE YOUNG FOALS AND MARES THAT ARE NURSING YOUNG.

Green Grass

GREEN GRASS IS THE HORSES NATURAL FOOD AND IT IS SUPPOSED TO CONTAIN MORE VITAMINS THAN ANY OTHER FORM OF VEGETATION. IF THE HORSE CAN'T BE TURNED OUT TO GRAZE, CUT GRASS MAY BE FED, BUT NEVER FEED GRASS THAT IS NOT FRESHLY CUT. GRASS THAT HAS BEEN ALLOWED TO LIE WITHOUT BEING PROPERLY CURED WILL FERMENT IN THE HORSE'S STOMACH AND CAUSE COLIC.

Salt

SALT
IN BLOCK
FORM.

SALT IS REQUIRED BY EVERY HORSE TO AID IN THE DIGESTION OF FOOD AND IN THE FORMATION OF BLOOD. WHEN SALT IS FED IN THE REGULAR DIET, NORMAL CONSUMPTION IS MAINTAINED, BUT IRREGULAR USE DEVELOPS ABNORMAL APPETITE FOR SALT WHICH RESULTS IN EXCESSIVE CONSUMPTION AND DIGESTIVE TROUBLES. AN AVERAGE HORSE WILL CONSUME UP TO 2 OUNCES OF SALT DAILY.

Water

THE AVERAGE HORSE WILL CONSUME 12 GALLONS OF WATER DAILY AND EVEN LARGER QUANTITIES IN HOT WEATHER. REGULARITY AND FREQUENT WATERING IS DESIRABLE, BUT IT IS DANGEROUS TO WATER HEAVILY A HORSE THAT IS HOT FROM EXERCISE. ALWAYS WATER BEFORE FEEDING. WATER DRUNK DIRECTLY AFTER A FEEDING WILL WASH FOOD THROUGH THE STOMACH BEFORE DIGESTION HAS OCCURRED.

Grooming Tools

THE STIFF WHISK FIBER DANDY BRUSH IS OFTEN USED FOR REMOVING MUD FROM THE COAT AND IS USEFUL FOR BRUSHING OUT THE MANE AND TAIL.

THE SOFT FIBER BODY BRUSH IS USED ON ANIMALS WITH SHORT OR CLIPPED COATS TO REMOVE DUST AND DIRT.

THE LIGHT WEIGHT ALUMINUM MANE COMB IS USED TO COMB OUT KNOTS IN THE MANE AND TAIL.

Grooming Tools

THE RUBBER CURRYCOMB IS USED TO REMOVE CAKED MUD AND LOOSEN MATTED SCURF AND DIRT.

THE ALUMINUM BODY-SCRAPER IS USED TO REMOVE SURPLUS WATER FROM THE BODY AFTER BATHING OR EXCESSIVE SWEATING.

THE STEEL HOOF PICK IS USED TO CLEAN OUT CAKED HOOFS AND FROG CLEFTS.

Grooming

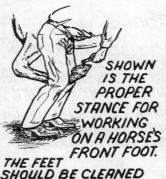

SHOWN IS THE PROPER STANCE FOR WORKING ON A HORSE'S FRONT FOOT.

THE FEET SHOULD BE CLEANED OUT EVERY TIME THE HORSE IS GROOMED.

GROOMING IS VERY ESSENTIAL TO THE GENERAL HEALTH AND APPEARANCE OF THE HORSE. A GOOD GROOMING CLEANS THE HAIR AND THE PORES OF THE SKIN SO THAT THE SKIN CAN PERFORM ITS NATURAL FUNCTIONS BETTER. A CLEAN AND HEALTHY SKIN IS LESS LIKELY TO BECOME INFESTED WITH SKIN PARASITES SUCH AS MITES AND LICE.

Bathing

BATHING A HORSE IS GOOD FOR HIM PROVIDING IT IS NOT DONE TO EXCESS. REMEMBER THAT THE HORSE CAN CATCH COLD IF BATHED IN COLD WEATHER OR WHILE STANDING IN A DRAFT. NEVER USE DETERGENTS AS THEY WILL IRRITATE THE SKIN. REGULAR FLEA SOAP FOR DOGS HAS BEEN FOUND SATISFACTORY. RINSE THE HORSE WELL AND THEN RUB DRY BEFORE PUTTING HIM AWAY.

FETLOCK CLIPPERS

← HAIR ON HEELS LEFT LONG.

Trimmed Fetlocks

THE FETLOCKS SHOULD ALWAYS BE KEPT TRIMMED, BUT THE BACK OF THE FETLOCK SHOULD NEVER BE CUT TOO CLOSE. IN COLD OR WET WEATHER THE LACK OF HAIR ON THE BACK OF FETLOCKS IS LIKELY TO CAUSE SCRATCHES. A MODERATE LENGTH OF HAIR OFFERS A NEAT APPEARANCE AND THE PROPER PROTECTION.

Bedding

A GOOD BED IN THE STALL CONTRIBUTES MUCH TO THE COMFORT AND EFFICIENCY OF THE HORSE. IT WILL INDUCE HIM TO LIE DOWN AND THUS GET BETTER REST. IT WILL HELP PREVENT BRUISING AND ABRASION OF THE ELBOWS, HOCK AND OTHER PARTS. DEEP BEDDING WILL ALSO KEEP HIS COAT CLEAN AND HELP TOWARD THE PREVENTION OF CONTRACTED HEELS. WHEAT STRAW MAKES THE BEST BEDDING. OAT AND BARLEY STRAW SHOULD BE AVOIDED.

Handling The Horse

Primitive Instinct

NEVER WALK UP ON A HORSE FROM BEHIND WITHOUT SPEAKING. A STARTLED HORSE MAY KICK OUT.

IN THE WILD STATE, THE HORSE WAS HIS OWN PROTECTOR AND HIS SURVIVAL OFTEN DEPENDED UPON HIS RAPIDITY OF ESCAPE. SUDDEN MOVEMENTS AND NOISES STILL ALARM HIM AND PRIMITIVE INSTINCT TELLS HIM TO RUN. THUS IT IS ALWAYS BEST WHEN WORKING AROUND ANY HORSE TO MOVE SLOWLY AND SPEAK IN A QUIET, CALM VOICE.

Training

WHIPPING A HORSE WILL NOT MAKE HIM RESPECT YOU, BUT IT CAN MAKE HIM HATE YOU.

TO TRAIN HORSES SUCCESSFULLY YOU NEED TO EXERCISE GREAT PATIENCE, GENTLENESS AND FIRMNESS. IF YOU ARE TRAINING A HORSE AND LOSE YOUR TEMPER, PUT THE ANIMAL IN THE STABLE UNTIL THE NEXT DAY. FURTHER WORK AT THIS TIME WOULD BE WORSE THAN USELESS AND COULD UNDO WORK ALREADY DONE. ABUSE YOUR HORSE AND YOU WILL ONLY ROB YOURSELF.

71

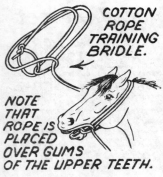

COTTON ROPE TRAINING BRIDLE.

NOTE THAT ROPE IS PLACED OVER GUMS OF THE UPPER TEETH.

A LIGHT JERKING WILL PUNISH THE HORSE IF HE RESISTS.

Instinct And Habit

MEMORY AND HABIT ARE THE TWO MAIN FACTORS WITH WHICH WE HAVE TO DEAL IN TRAINING HORSES. A HORSE ACTS THROUGH INSTINCT AND HABIT, ASSOCIATED WITH THE MEMORY OF WHAT HE HAS FORMERLY LEARNED. ONE OF THE GREATEST CHARACTERISTICS OF THE HORSE IS HIS UNIFORMITY OF CONDUCT, FOR WHAT HE HAS ONCE BEEN TRAINED TO DO, HE WILL NEARLY ALWAYS DO UNDER LIKE CONDITIONS.

HORSES WILL NORMALLY RESPOND QUICKLY TO A GENTLE HAND AND FRIENDLY VOICE.

Rewards

A PRAISING VOICE AND GENTLE PAT ARE THE TWO MOST COMMON REWARDS GIVEN THE HORSE. A LUMP OF SUGAR OR A CARROT ARE ALSO EFFECTIVE REWARDS, BUT CAN MAKE FOR GREAT DISAPPOINTMENT IF THEY ARE NOT ALWAYS AVAILABLE. TO BE EFFECTIVE ALL REWARDS SHOULD BE GIVEN ONLY WHEN THEY ARE DESERVED.

72

Temperament

A NERVOUS, EXCITABLE HORSE IS USUALLY DIFFICULT TO CONTROL, BUT THEN A SLUGGISH, PHLEGMATIC ONE LACKS AMBITION AND ENDURANCE. GENERALLY A DESIRABLE TEMPERAMENT IS INDICATED BY LARGE, MILD, BRIGHT EYES, WILLING OBEDIENCE AND AN ALERT, GRACEFUL MOVING BODY.

EYES SET FAR OUT AND FURROWS OR WRINKLES BETWEEN THE EYES WILL OFTEN INDICATE A NERVOUS DISPOSITION AND GREAT AMBITION.

SHOWN BELOW IS A METHOD OF THROWING THE HORSE.

Restraint

WHEN HANDLING HORSES SPECIAL RESTRAINT IS SOMETIMES NECESSARY. ALWAYS TRY TO SELECT THE MILDEST METHOD AND THE LEAST DANGEROUS FOR BOTH MAN AND THE ANIMAL. ALWAYS KEEP IN MIND THAT KINDNESS, TACT AND PERSEVERANCE WILL OFTEN ACCOMPLISH THE DESIRED PURPOSE WITHOUT USING A SPECIAL MEANS OF RESTRAINT.

LEAD ROPE SNAPPED TO THE HALTER.

KNEE STRAP.

PULL HARD.

73

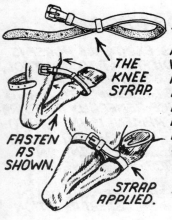

Knee Strap

THE KNEE STRAP.

FASTEN AS SHOWN.

STRAP APPLIED.

IN SHOEING THE HORSE OR OFTEN WHEN JUST WORKING ON HIM, IT MAY BE FOUND NECESSARY TO FIX A FORELEG. A STRAP ABOUT 3 FEET LONG IS SOMETIMES USED TO FASTEN THE PASTERN TO THE FOREARM. FIRST FASTEN THE STRAP AROUND THE PASTERN, THEN BEND THE LEG AND PULL THE STRAP END AROUND THE FOREARM AND BUCKLE IT.

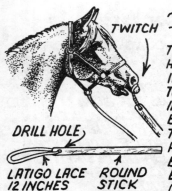

Nose Twitch

TWITCH

DRILL HOLE

LATIGO LACE 12 INCHES LONG.

ROUND STICK 2 FEET LONG.

THE TWITCH IS THE SIMPLEST AND HANDIEST METHOD OF SPECIAL RESTRAINT. IT IS NOT USED TO HURT THE HORSE, BUT TO CENTER HIS ATTENTION ON HIS LIP INSTEAD OF ON WHATEVER ELSE IS BEING DONE TO HIM. ALTHOUGH THE TWITCH SHOULD BE USED WITH CAUTION AND ONLY WHEN NECESSARY, IT CAN BE A PRICELESS PIECE OF STABLE EQUIPMENT WHEN TRYING TO DOCTOR OR SHOE A TOUCHY HORSE. MAKE YOUR OWN TWITCH AS SHOWN.

PRESS BARS WITH THUMB AND INDEX FINGER OF LEFT HAND, LIFT THE BRIDLE WITH RIGHT HAND.

Refusing The Bit

MANY HORSES WILL REFUSE TO TAKE THE BIT. IN SUCH CASES IT IS NECESSARY TO PRESS ON THE BARS OF THE MOUTH WITH YOUR FINGERS. THIS PRESSURE SELDOM FAILS TO OPEN EVEN THE MOST STUBBORN MOUTH. SLIP THE BIT IN GENTLY, NEVER SLAM IT AGAINST THE ANIMAL'S TEETH. SUCH ROUGHNESS IS OFTEN THE CAUSE OF A HORSE'S REFUSING TO TAKE THE BIT.

TESTING TIGHTNESS OF GIRTH.

IF THE FINGERS CAN NOT BE INSERTED BETWEEN HORSE AND GIRTH, IT IS TOO TIGHT.

Girth Tightness

BE SURE THAT YOUR SADDLE IS CINCHED TIGHT ENOUGH TO PREVENT ITS TURNING WHEN MOUNTING OR MOVING WHEN THE HORSE IS IN MOTION. BUT A CINCH TOO TIGHT INTERFERES WITH BREATHING AND ADDS TO PRESSURE ON THE HORSE'S BACK. ON LONG RIDES OCCASIONAL LOOSENING OF THE CINCH AND RE-SETTING THE SADDLE WILL HELP PREVENT SADDLE SORES.

Lever System

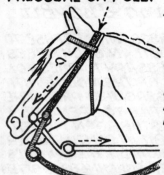

PRESSURE ON POLL.

THE ACCOMPANYING DRAWING SHOWS THE SYSTEM OF LEVERS CALLED THE BIT AND BRIDLE. TENSION ON THE REINS PULLS BACK THE BRANCH OF THE BIT. NOTICE THAT AS THE BIT IS PULLED BACK, THE CHEEK PIECE OF THE BRIDLE IS PULLED DOWN. THIS PRESSURE ON THE POLL, WHICH AFFECTS THE SENSITIVE NERVES, TENDS TO STOP THE HORSE AS MUCH AS THE BIT.

The Walk

THE NORMAL GAITS

WALK — 4 MPH

TROT — 8 MPH

GALLOP — 12 MPH

EACH AND EVERY RIDE SHOULD BEGIN WITH A PERIOD OF AT LEAST 10 MINUTES AT A WALK SO THAT GOOD CIRCULATION MAY BE ESTABLISHED. THE RIDE SHOULD ALSO END AT A WALK SO THE HORSE WILL BE DRY AND BREATHING NORMALLY WHEN HE REACHES THE STABLE. THE WALK IS THE PRIME CONDITIONING GAIT AND THE ONLY ONE THAT IS RARELY OVERUSED.

76

Work After Eating

A HORSE SHOULD NEVER BE WORKED DIRECTLY AFTER EATING A FULL MEAL. AFTER A FULL MEAL, THE HORSE'S STOMACH AND BOWELS ARE DISTENDED AND CONTAIN MORE GASES, RESULTING FROM DIGESTION. THE SIZE OF THE THORACIC CAVITY IS THUS REDUCED AND THE LUNGS ARE PREVENTED FROM EXPANDING TO THEIR CAPACITY. WAIT AT LEAST ONE HOUR AFTER THE HORSE HAS EATEN TO EXERCISE OR WORK HIM.

DIGESTIVE DISORDERS OR EVEN DEATH CAN RESULT FROM HARD WORK AFTER A MEAL.

Shying

WHEN THE HORSE SHYS AWAY FROM AN OBJECT, NEVER WHIP HIM. IN HIS MIND THE PAIN CAUSED BY THE WHIP WILL BE ASSOCIATED WITH THE OBJECT THAT MADE HIM SHY, THERE-FORE THE NEXT TIME HE SEES THE SAME OBJECT HE WILL EXPECT THE PAIN AND SHY. WITH A PRAISING VOICE AND GENTLE PATS, ENCOURAGE THE HORSE TO EXAMINE THE OBJECT.

A WHIP WILL OFTEN MAKE MATTERS WORSE.

77

Bolting

SHOULD YOUR HORSE BOLT AND RUN AT HIGH SPEED, DON'T PANIC. TO SLOW HIM DOWN PULL ON THE REINS ALTERNATELY WITH SHORT, HARD JERKS. PULL THE ANIMAL'S HEAD SIDEWAYS AND TRY TO GET HIM GOING IN A CIRCLE. IF YOU ARE IN ROUGH COUNTRY TURN HIM INTO A STEEP EARTH BANK.

NEVER PULL ON BOTH REINS AT ONCE. TO SOME HORSES A STEADY, HARD PULL IS A SIGNAL FOR SPEED.

WHILE THE HORSE IS SHAKING HIS HEAD TO FREE HIS EAR...

Balking

URGE HIM FORWARD.

WHIPPING A BALKY HORSE WILL ONLY ANGER HIM AND MAKE MATTERS WORSE. THE RIDER SHOULD TRY TO GET THE ANIMAL'S MIND OFF THE IDEA OF HIS RESISTANCE. THIS CAN OFTEN BE DONE BY TUCKING AN EAR UNDER THE BROWBAND OF THE BRIDLE. THE HORSE WILL SHAKE HIS HEAD TO FREE THE EAR AND IN DOING SO WILL FORGET HIS DECISION TO BALK.

78

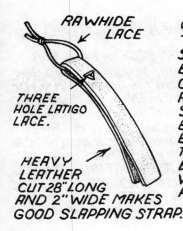

RAWHIDE LACE

THREE HOLE LATIGO LACE.

HEAVY LEATHER CUT 28" LONG AND 2" WIDE MAKES GOOD SLAPPING STRAP.

Biting

SOME HORSES DEVELOP THE BAD HABIT OF NIPPING YOUR CLOTHES OR REACHING AROUND AND BITING YOUR FOOT IN THE STIRRUP. THIS CUTE HABIT CAN BECOME DANGEROUS AND SHOULD BE STOPPED. A LOUD SLAP ON THE NECK WITH A WIDE STRAP EACH TIME THE ANIMAL NIPS WILL SOON DISCOURAGE THE HABIT.

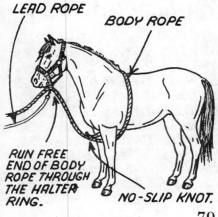

LEAD ROPE

BODY ROPE

RUN FREE END OF BODY ROPE THROUGH THE HALTER RING.

NO-SLIP KNOT.

Halter Pulling

PULLING BACK AND BREAKING THE HALTER IS A BAD HABIT ENCOUNTERED IN TOO MANY HORSES. A GOOD REMEDY FOR THIS IS THE USE OF A BODY ROPE APPLIED AS ILLUSTRATED. A FEW DAYS' EXPERIENCE WITH THE BODY ROPE WILL USUALLY PUT AN END TO BROKEN HALTERS.

79

Trailer Loading

SHOWN BELOW IS A METHOD OF DOUBLE TYING A HORSE IN THE TRAILER.

BECAUSE THE TRAILER RAMP SOUNDS STRANGE AND GIVES THE HORSE A SENSE OF INSECURITY, THERE IS OFTEN RELUCTANCE TO ENTER THE TRAILER. ALLOW THE HORSE TO EXAMINE THE TRAILER AND AVOID ANY EXCITEMENT OR NOISE. ONLY A GENTLE INTRO- DUCTION TO THE TRAILER WILL RESULT IN THE HORSE'S BECOMING ACCUSTOMED TO IT.

Transportation

HORSES TRANSPORTED IN OPEN TRAILERS SHOULD WEAR GOGGLES TO PROTECT THEIR EYES FROM DIRT AND BUGS IN THE AIR.

WHEN TRANSPORTING A HORSE ALWAYS REMEMBER, THAT LIKE HUMANS, THE HORSE NEEDS TO REST AND STRETCH HIS LEGS. BECAUSE STANDING FOR LONG PERIODS REDUCES CIRCULATION, IT SHOULD ALSO BE REMEMBERED NEVER TO OVER-EXERCISE THE HORSE AFTER A LONG JOURNEY. GIVE HIM AT LEAST 2 HOURS' REST.

80

General Information

Fire

WE MUST BEAR IN MIND THAT HORSES
WILL NOT NORMALLY LEAVE A BURN-
ING STABLE OF THEIR OWN VOLITION.
CUTTING THEM LOOSE IS NOT ENOUGH.
LOOSE ANIMALS GENERALLY CAN'T
BE HERDED FROM A BURNING BARN,
BUT MUST BE LED TO SAFETY. IN
SOME CASES A BLINDFOLD MAY
BE NECESSARY. IF TURNED LOOSE
OUTSIDE THEY MIGHT ATTEMPT TO
RETURN TO THEIR STALLS.

Muzzle

LACE HEAVY LEATHER

MANY HORSES PERSIST IN CHEWING
UP THEIR COOLING SHEETS OR WINTER
BLANKETS. THE SIMPLE MUZZLE SHOWN
WILL MAKE IT ALMOST IMPOSSIBLE
FOR THEM TO GET THEIR TEETH INTO
THE BLANKET, YET THE LEATHER
WILL GIVE ENOUGH TO ALLOW
THEM TO EAT OR DRINK UNHINDERED.
USE A HEAVY PIECE OF LEATHER,
PUNCH HOLES AS ILLUSTRATED
AND TIE TO THE HALTER RINGS
WITH PIECES OF RAWHIDE LACE.

Indian Bridle

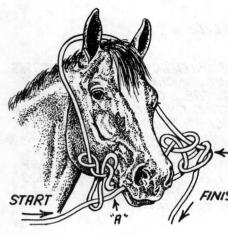

THIS INDIAN BRIDLE IS STILL USED BY MANY OF TODAY'S HORSEMEN. IT MAY LOOK DIFFICULT, BUT WITH A LITTLE PRACTICE IT BECOMES EASY.

THE ROPE IS SHOWN LOOSELY CONSTRUCTED FOR CLARITY.

BY PLACING THE MOUTH-PIECE "A" OVER THE NOSE THE BRIDLE SERVES AS A HALTER.

START

"A"

FINISH

Orphan Foal

ARTIFICIAL FEEDING OF A FOAL MAY BECOME NECESSARY DUE TO THE DEATH OF THE MOTHER OR DISEASE WHICH MAY RENDER THE MOTHER'S MILK DANGEROUS. COW'S MILK MAY BE USED AND MIXED AS DESCRIBED. COW'S MILK 3 PARTS; LIME WATER, 1 PART; AND 1 TABLESPOONFUL OF SUGAR TO ½ PINT OF MIXTURE. TWO OUNCES AT BODY TEMPERATURE SHOULD BE GIVEN EVERY 2 HOURS. INCREASE AMOUNT AS THE FOAL BECOMES OLDER.

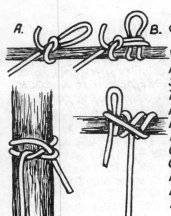

Secure Knots

A. B.

WHETHER HORSES ARE TIED TO A TREE, HITCHING RAIL OR POST, THE TIE ROPE SHOULD BE OF PROPER LENGTH AND THE KNOT SECURE. LONG TIE ROPES RESULT IN ROPE BURNS AND LEG INJURIES. INSECURE KNOTS RESULT IN LOOSE HORSES. A SECURE KNOT ON A TIE ROPE SHOULD ALSO BE ONE THAT CAN BE UNTIED RAPIDLY IN CASE OF EMERGENCY. THREE EASILY UNTIED, SECURE KNOTS ARE ILLUSTRATED.

The Pigtail Knot

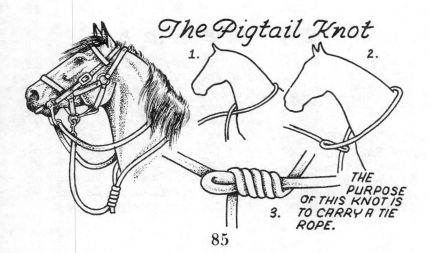

1.

2.

3.

THE PURPOSE OF THIS KNOT IS TO CARRY A TIE ROPE.

85

Respiration

133.55
CUBIC FEET

WALK

849.10
CUBIC FEET

GALLOP

THE LUNGS OF THE AVERAGE HORSE WHEN FREELY DISTENDED, CONTAIN 1½ CUBIC FEET OF AIR. THE NORMAL HORSE AT REST BREATHES FROM 8-16 TIMES PER MINUTE AND INHALES AT EACH RESPIRATION APPROXIMATELY 250 CUBIC INCHES OF AIR. WALKING HE NEARLY TREBLES THE NUMBER OF NORMAL RESPIRATIONS, BUT IT IS REGAINED A FEW MINUTES AFTER STOPPING.

The Brain

CONTRARY TO BELIEF, THE SKULL OF THE HORSE IS NOT ONE SINGLE BONE, BUT IS MADE UP OF 30 SEPARATE BONES.

IN PROPORTION TO BODY SIZE, THE BRAIN OF THE HORSE IS QUITE SMALL WHEN COMPARED WITH THAT OF A DOG. DEPEND-ING UPON THE BREED, WEIGHT OF THE BRAIN MAY BE FROM ½ TO 1 PER CENT OF THE DOG'S WEIGHT, WHILE IN THE HORSE IT IS ONLY 1/7 OF ONE PER CENT IN A MEDIUM SIZE ANIMAL.

86

The Corral

FENCES CONSTRUCTED OF WOOD POSTS AND RAILS SHOULD ALWAYS HAVE THE POSTS SET ON THE OUTSIDE.

THE CORRAL SHOULD BE CLEANED AT LEAST EVERY SECOND DAY AND ALL DEPRESSIONS KEPT FILLED SO THAT POOLS OF WATER WILL NOT FORM AFTER A RAIN. THE FENCE SHOULD BE OF SUFFICIENT HEIGHT AND STRONG ENOUGH TO RESTRAIN THE HORSE. ALL FENCING SHOULD ALWAYS BE KEPT IN A THOROUGH STATE OF REPAIR.

Saddle Rack

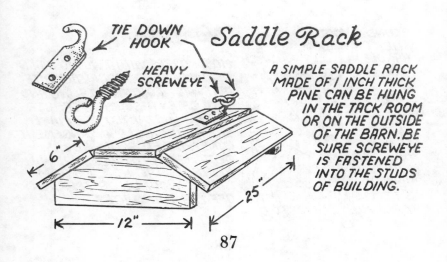

TIE DOWN HOOK

HEAVY SCREWEYE

A SIMPLE SADDLE RACK MADE OF 1 INCH THICK PINE CAN BE HUNG IN THE TACK ROOM OR ON THE OUTSIDE OF THE BARN. BE SURE SCREWEYE IS FASTENED INTO THE STUDS OF BUILDING.

6"

25"

12"

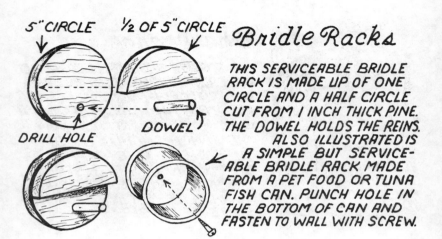

Bridle Racks

THIS SERVICEABLE BRIDLE RACK IS MADE UP OF ONE CIRCLE AND A HALF CIRCLE CUT FROM 1 INCH THICK PINE. THE DOWEL HOLDS THE REINS.

ALSO ILLUSTRATED IS A SIMPLE BUT SERVICEABLE BRIDLE RACK MADE FROM A PET FOOD OR TUNA FISH CAN. PUNCH HOLE IN THE BOTTOM OF CAN AND FASTEN TO WALL WITH SCREW.

5" CIRCLE

½ OF 5" CIRCLE

DRILL HOLE

DOWEL

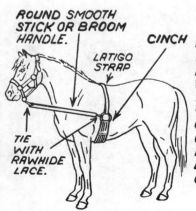

No-Bite

ROUND SMOOTH STICK OR BROOM HANDLE.

LATIGO STRAP

CINCH

TIE WITH RAWHIDE LACE.

MOST HORSES WITH A WOUND WITHIN REACH OF THEIR TEETH WILL BITE AT IT. THIS PROLONGS HEALING AND WILL OFTEN RESULT IN A LARGER SCAR. ILLUSTRATED IS A MAKESHIFT SURCINGLE ARRANGEMENT, CONSTRUCTED FROM EASILY OBTAINED MATERIALS, THAT WILL RESTRAIN THE HORSE FROM BITING WOUNDS OR TEARING OFF LEG BANDAGES.

USE A SOFT
COTTON ROPE.

A ROPE
AROUND HINDQUARTERS
TEACHES COLT TO LEAD.

Educate Early

IT IS A GREAT ADVANTAGE TO BEGIN
THE EDUCATION OF A COLT AS EARLY
AS POSSIBLE. HANDLE AND PET, BUT
NEVER ROUGH HIM. IT IS A GOOD IDEA
TO BREAK THE COLT TO LEAD BEFORE
HE IS WEANED. ACCUSTOM COLTS
TO WORK GRADUALLY. DEVELOPING
A COLT INTO A SOUND, HEALTHY
HORSE THROUGH PROPER TRAINING
AND CARE SHOULD BE THE OBJECT
OF EVERY HORSEMAN.

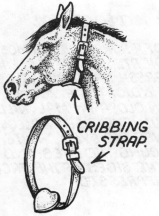

CRIBBING
STRAP.

Cribbing

WHEN A HORSE BITES HARD ON
THE MANGER WHILE STRAINING
MUSCLES OF HIS NECK AND
SUCKING AIR, IT IS CALLED
CRIBBING. SOME SAY THAT
THIS HABIT IS CAUSED FROM
GAS ON THE STOMACH OR
NERVOUSNESS. ALTHOUGH THERE
IS NO KNOWN CURE IT CAN BE
PREVENTED BY A STRAP BUCKLED
AROUND THE THROAT.

89

Chewing Wood

MANY HORSES DEVELOP THE HABIT OF CHEWING WOOD. SOME SAY THAT IT IS CAUSED BY NERVOUSNESS OR A DIETARY DEFICIENCY. BUT MANY TIMES IT IS BROUGHT ON BY BOREDOM. THE HABIT RESULTS IN COSTLY REPAIRS AND THE WOOD SPLINTERS CAN DO SERIOUS HARM TO THE INTESTINES. THE APPLICATION OF CREOSOTE TO CHEWED AREAS WILL DISCOURAGE MOST HORSES. METAL STRIPS NAILED TO WOOD EDGES WILL ALSO HELP.

Age Indication

THE HEAD OF A HORSE WILL IN MOST CASES INDICATE ITS AGE. A CLEAR EYE AND FRESH APPEARANCE OF THE HEAD INDICATES A YOUNG ANIMAL. AN OLDER ANIMAL WILL SHOW A DULL EYE, DEEP HOLLOW PLACES OVER THE EYES, WHITE HAIRS AROUND THE EYES AND MUZZLE. THE SIDES OF THE FACE WILL BE DEPRESSED.

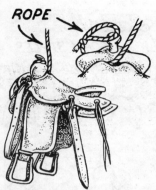

ROPE

SIMPLE METHOD TO
HANG SADDLE.

Neatsfoot Oil

NEATSFOOT OIL IS HIGHLY RECOM-
MENDED FOR LEATHER, BUT IT CAN
BE MESSY UNLESS CARE IS TAKEN
TO REMOVE ALL THE EXCESS AFTER
APPLICATION. A FEW DAYS AFTER
OILING, GO OVER THE LEATHER
WITH SADDLE SOAP. WORK HEAVY
DRY LATHER INTO LEATHER AND
THEN BUFF DRY WITH SOFT CLOTH.
APPLY NEATSFOOT OIL ABOUT 3
TIMES A YEAR TO ALL TACK.

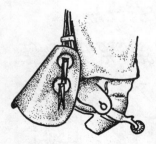

TAPADEROS OR ANY
LEATHER COVERED
STIRRUP WILL KEEP
FEET WARMER.

Winter Riding

HORSEMEN IN THE SNOW COUNTRY
WHO RIDE IN THE WINTER USUALLY
HAVE TROUBLE WITH SNOW BALL-
ING UP IN THEIR HORSES' FEET.
THIS TROUBLESOME CONDITION
CAN BE HELPED BY SMEARING A
GENEROUS LAYER OF VASELINE
ON THE ENTIRE GROUND SURFACE
OF THE HORSES' FEET. THIS WILL
HELP KEEP THEM FREE OF SNOW
FOR AS LONG AS ONE HOUR.

The Western Saddle

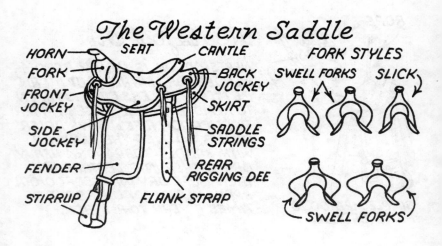

HORN
FORK
FRONT JOCKEY
SIDE JOCKEY
FENDER
STIRRUP

SEAT
CANTLE
BACK JOCKEY
SKIRT
SADDLE STRINGS
REAR RIGGING DEE
FLANK STRAP

FORK STYLES
SWELL FORKS — SLICK
SWELL FORKS

The Latigo Hitch

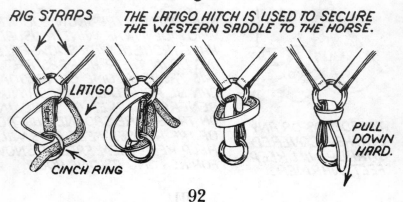

RIG STRAPS

THE LATIGO HITCH IS USED TO SECURE THE WESTERN SADDLE TO THE HORSE.

LATIGO
CINCH RING
PULL DOWN HARD.

Saddle Riggings

SHOWN ARE THE
RIGGINGS USED ON
TODAY'S WESTERN
SADDLES.

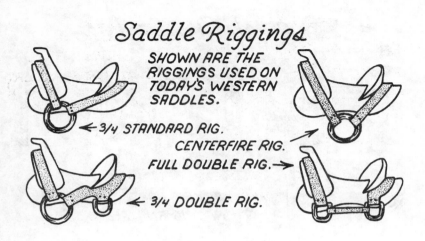

← 3/4 STANDARD RIG.

CENTERFIRE RIG.

FULL DOUBLE RIG. →

← 3/4 DOUBLE RIG.

Western Bit Styles

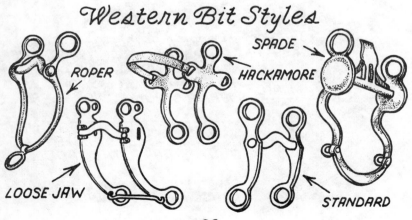

SPADE →

ROPER

HACKAMORE

LOOSE JAW

STANDARD

93

English Bit Styles

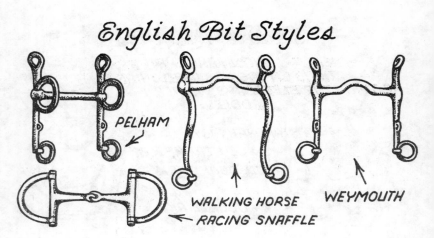

PELHAM

WALKING HORSE
RACING SNAFFLE

WEYMOUTH

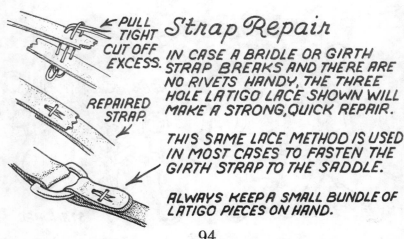

PULL
TIGHT

CUT OFF
EXCESS.

REPAIRED
STRAP.

Strap Repair

IN CASE A BRIDLE OR GIRTH
STRAP BREAKS AND THERE ARE
NO RIVETS HANDY, THE THREE
HOLE LATIGO LACE SHOWN WILL
MAKE A STRONG, QUICK REPAIR.

THIS SAME LACE METHOD IS USED
IN MOST CASES TO FASTEN THE
GIRTH STRAP TO THE SADDLE.

ALWAYS KEEP A SMALL BUNDLE OF
LATIGO PIECES ON HAND.

The Bleed Knot

OFTEN THERE ARE THOSE WHO WANT TO REPLACE OLD, WORN LATIGOS ON THEIR TACK, BUT ARE CONFUSED IN RE-TYING THE BLEED KNOT.

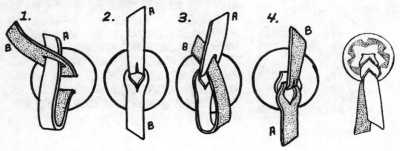

Markings

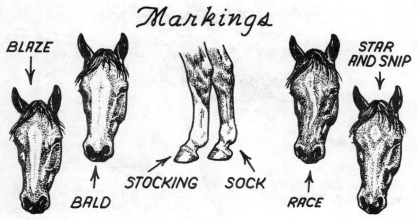

BLAZE

BALD

STOCKING   SOCK

RACE

STAR AND SNIP

USE A MEASURING STICK
OR TAPE.

Measuring

THE HEIGHT OF A HORSE IS DETERMINED
BY MEASURING THE VERTICAL DISTANCE
FROM THE HIGHEST POINT OF HIS
WITHERS TO THE GROUND. THE UNIT OF
MEASUREMENT USED IN EXPRESSING
A HORSE'S HEIGHT IS THE HAND, EACH
HAND CONSIDERED FOUR INCHES. FOR
EXAMPLE A HORSE MEASURING 60
INCHES AT THE WITHERS IS 15 HANDS
TALL. ANY HORSE STANDING LESS
THAN 14.2 HANDS IS CLASSED AS
A PONY.

Horseshoeing Tools

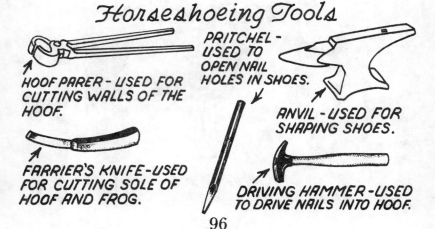

HOOF PARER - USED FOR
CUTTING WALLS OF THE
HOOF.

FARRIER'S KNIFE - USED
FOR CUTTING SOLE OF
HOOF AND FROG.

PRITCHEL -
USED TO
OPEN NAIL
HOLES IN SHOES.

ANVIL - USED FOR
SHAPING SHOES.

DRIVING HAMMER - USED
TO DRIVE NAILS INTO HOOF.

EMERGENCY ROPE HALTERS

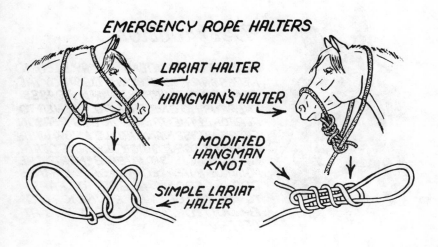

LARIAT HALTER

HANGMAN'S HALTER

MODIFIED HANGMAN KNOT

SIMPLE LARIAT HALTER

EMERGENCY ROPE BRIDLES

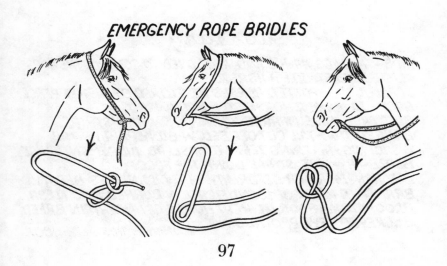

Destruction

IN CASE OF ACCIDENT IT MAY BECOME NECESSARY TO QUICKLY DESTROY THE SUFFERING ANIMAL. IN MANY CASES THERE IS NO ONE BUT THE OWNER TO PERFORM THE TASK. FOR THIS REASON EVERY HORSEMAN SHOULD KNOW WHERE TO SHOOT FOR A QUICK, HUMANE DEATH. THE BRAIN IS SITUATED BENEATH THE POINT OF INTERSECTION OF TWO LINES DRAWN FROM THE BASE OF EARS TO THE TOP OF EYES AS INDICATED BY DOTTED LINES IN DRAWING AT LEFT.

Glossary

AIDS - THE LEGS, HANDS AND VOICE, USED TO CONTROL THE HORSE.
ALTER - TO CASTRATE A HORSE.
APPALOOSA - SPOTTED HORSES DEVELOPED BY THE NEZ PERCE.
BACK - TO MAKE A HORSE STEP BACKWARDS.
BALD FACE - FACE MARKED WITH WIDE WHITE STRIPE.
BANGED TAIL - TAIL CUT OFF BELOW BONY PART OF TAIL.
BISHOPING - ALTERING TEETH TO MISLEAD JUDGEMENT OF AGE.
BLAZE - A WHITE STRIPE DOWN THE FACE.
BLEMISH - MARK OR DEFORMITY THAT DIMINISHES BEAUTY.
BRAND - A MARK OF IDENTIFICATION BURNED INTO FLESH.
BROOM TAIL - POOR, ILL-KEPT HORSE OF UNCERTAIN BREED.
BUCKEYED - EYE PROTRUDING.

CALF-KNEED - FORELEGS APPEAR TO BEND BACK AT KNEES.
CANNON- THE LEG BONE BELOW THE KNEE AND HOCK.
CANTER- MODERATE, EASY COLLECTED GALLOP.
CAVY- A COLLECTION OF HORSES.
CAYUSE - AN INDIAN PONY.
CENTER FIRE - CINCH HUNG FROM CENTER OF WESTERN SADDLE.
CHESTNUTS - HORNY GROWTHS ON THE INSIDE OF LEGS.
CINCH - WIDE CORD GIRTH USED ON WESTERN SADDLES.
CLEVER - A GENTLE, GOOD -NATURED HORSE.
COB - A STYLISH, HIGH-ACTIONED HORSE.
COLD -BLOODED -HORSE WITH ANCESTRY FROM THE BIG-
      HEADED NORTHERN RACES OF HORSES.
COLT - A MALE FOAL.
COMBINATION HORSE - ONE USED FOR RIDING AND DRIVING.

CONFORMATION - STRUCTURE AND FORM OF THE HORSE.
COW-HOCKED -HOCKS CLOSE TOGETHER, FEET WIDE APART.
CREST- UPPER CURVED PART OF THE NECK.
CROSS - A DARK STRIPE ACROSS THE SHOULDERS.
CROSSBRED - DAM AND SIRE OF DIFFERENT BREED.
CROW HOPS - MILD BUCKING MOTIONS.
CURB - A TYPE BIT USED TO RESTRAIN THE HORSE.
DAM - THE FEMALE PARENT OF A HORSE.
DRESSAGE - ADVANCED TRAINING IN HORSEMANSHIP.
EWE-NECKED - TOP PROFILE OF NECK CONCAVE.
FAVOR - TO LIMP SLIGHTLY.
FERAL - A WILD HORSE.
FILLY - A FEMALE FOAL.
FLAME - A FEW WHITE HAIRS IN CENTER OF FOREHEAD.

FLAT-FOOT - WHEN THE FOOT ANGLE IS LESS THAN 45 DEGREES.
FLOATING - FILING ROUGH TEETH.
FOAL - A COLT OR FILLY UNDER NINE MONTHS OLD.
FOREFOOTING - ROPING A HORSE BY THE FOREFEET.
FORGING - THE TOE OF THE REAR FOOT STRIKING THE FOREFOOT.
GAITS - THE MANNER OF GOING OF A HORSE.
GELD - TO CUT OR CASTRATE A HORSE.
GELDING - AN ALTERED HORSE.
GET - THE PROGENY OF A STALLION.
GLASS EYE - A BLUE OR WHITISH COLORED EYE.
GOOSE-RUMPED - A NARROW, DROOPING RUMP.
GREEN HORSE - ONE WITH LITTLE TRAINING.
GYMKHANA - GAMES PLAYED FROM HORSEBACK.
HACKAMORE - A BITLESS BRIDLE DESIGNED FOR TRAINING.

HAND - A MEASURE OF THE HEIGHT OF HORSES.
HEAD SHY - A HORSE THAT IS SENSITIVE ABOUT HIS HEAD.
HEAD STALL - LEATHER BRIDLE EXCLUSIVE OF BIT AND REINS.
HERD BOUND - A HORSE WHO REFUSES TO LEAVE OTHER HORSES.
HIGH SCHOOL - ADVANCED TRAINING OF THE HORSE.
HOGGED - A SHORT-CUT MANE.
LEAD - THE FIRST STRIDE IN THE CANTER.
LONGE - A LONG LINE ATTACHED TO A HALTER FOR TRAINING.
MARE - A FEMALE HORSE.
NEAR SIDE - THE LEFT SIDE.
OFF SIDE - THE RIGHT SIDE.
OUTLAW - A HORSE THAT CANNOT BE BROKEN.
PIEBALD - HORSE OF BLACK AND WHITE SPOTS.
PINTO - A HORSE OF BROWN AND WHITE SPOTS.

100

POLL-THE TOP OF A HORSE'S HEAD JUST BACK OF THE EARS.
PONY-ANY HORSE MEASURING UNDER 14.2 HANDS TALL.
PORT-MOUTHPIECE OF A BIT CURVING UP OVER THE TONGUE.
POUNDING-STRIKING GROUND HARD IN THE STRIDE.
PUREBRED-HORSE WITH ANCESTRY OF DEFINITE BREED.
RAY - A BLACK LINE ALONG THE SPINE.
ROACHED BACK - A THIN, ARCHED BACK.
SCALPING-HITTING CORONET OF HIND FOOT AGAINST THE
          TOE OF FRONT FOOT.
SKEWBALD-HORSE WITH BROWN, WHITE AND BLACK SPOTS.
SNIP- A WHITE STREAK ON THE NOSE.
SPREAD- TO STRETCH OUT OR POSE.
STALLION- UNALTERED MALE HORSE.
STAR - WHITE SPOT IN CENTER OF FOREHEAD.

STARGAZER-A HORSE THAT HOLDS HIS HEAD TOO HIGH.
STRIDE-THE DISTANCE BETWEEN PRINTS OF SAME FOOT.
SUNFISHER-A BUCKING HORSE THAT TWISTS HIS BODY.
SURCINGLE-A BROAD STRAP ABOUT THE GIRTH.
TACK- SADDLES AND BRIDLES.
TACK UP - TO SADDLE AND BRIDLE THE HORSE.
THINNED TAIL-HAIRS OF TAIL HAVE BEEN PULLED OUT.
TRAPPY - A HIGH, QUICK STRIDE.
TUCKED UP-A THIN HORSE CUT UP IN THE FLANK.
WALLEYED - IRIS OF THE EYE A LIGHT COLOR.
WAR BRIDLE -AN EMERGENCY BRIDLE MADE OF ROPE.
WRANGLING - ROUNDING UP RANGE HORSES.
ZEBRA- PARALLEL DARK MARKINGS ON THE LEGS.

Breed Registries

THE AMERICAN ALBINO
NAPER, NEBRASKA

ARABIAN HORSE REGISTRY
CHICAGO, ILLINOIS

APPALOOSA HORSE CLUB
MOSCOW, IDAHO

AMERICAN HACKNEY HORSE
FAIR LAWN, NEW JERSEY

AMERICAN SADDLE HORSE
929 SOUTH FOURTH ST.
LOUISVILLE, KENTUCKY

HALF ARABIAN REGISTRY
224 EAST OLIVE AVE.
BURBANK, CALIFORNIA

MORGAN HORSE CLUB
WEST HARTFORD 17, CONN.

PALOMINO HORSE
CHATSWOURTH, CALIF.

MOROCCO SPOTTED HORSE
GREENFIELD, IOWA

SPANISH MUSTANG REGISTRY
FINLEY, OKLAHOMA

PINTO HORSE ASSOCIATION
BOX 155 RFD#1 SOMERS Rd.
ELLINGTON, CONNECTICUT

TENNESSEE WALKING HORSE
P.O. BOX 87
LEWISBURG, TENNESSEE

AMERICAN QUARTER HORSE
AMARILLO, TEXAS

WELSH PONY SOCIETY
EDWARDSVILLE, VIRGINIA

AMERICAN SHETLAND PONY
BOX 648
LAFAYETTE, INDIANA

STANDARDBRED REGISTRY
750 MICHIGAN AVE.
COLUMBUS 15, OHIO

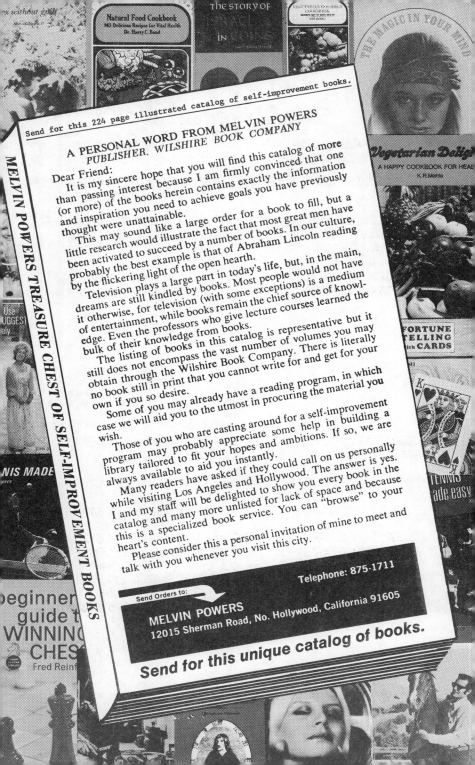

Melvin Powers
SELF-IMPROVEMENT
LIBRARY

ABILITY TO LOVE *Dr. Allan Fromme*	$2.00
ACT YOUR WAY TO SUCCESSFUL LIVING *Neil & Margaret Rau*	2.00
ADVANCED TECHNIQUES OF HYPNOSIS *Melvin Powers*	1.00
ANIMAL HYPNOSIS *Dr. F. A. Völgyesi*	2.00
ASTROLOGY: A FASCINATING HISTORY *P. Naylor*	2.00
ASTROLOGY: HOW TO CHART YOUR HOROSCOPE *Max Heindel*	2.00
ASTROLOGY: YOUR PERSONAL SUN-SIGN GUIDE *Beatrice Ryder*	2.00
ASTROLOGY FOR EVERYDAY LIVING *Janet Harris*	2.00
ASTROLOGY GUIDE TO GOOD HEALTH *Alexandra Kayhle*	2.00
ASTROLOGY MADE EASY *Astarte*	2.00
ASTROLOGY MADE PRACTICAL *Alexandra Kayhle*	2.00
ASTROLOGY, ROMANCE, YOU AND THE STARS *Anthony Novell*	2.00
BEGINNER'S GUIDE TO WINNING CHESS *Fred Reinfeld*	2.00
BETTER CHESS — How to Play *Fred Reinfeld*	2.00
BICYCLING FOR FUN AND GOOD HEALTH *Kenneth E. Luther*	2.00
BOOK OF TALISMANS, AMULETS & ZODIACAL GEMS *William Pavitt*	3.00
BRIDGE BIDDING MADE EASY *Edwin Kantar*	5.00
BRIDGE CONVENTIONS *Edwin Kantar*	4.00
CHECKERS MADE EASY *Tom Wiswell*	2.00
CHESS IN TEN EASY LESSONS *Larry Evans*	2.00
CHESS MADE EASY *Milton L. Hanauer*	2.00
CHESS MASTERY — A New Approach *Fred Reinfeld*	2.00
CHESS PROBLEMS FOR BEGINNERS *edited by Fred Reinfeld*	2.00
CHESS SECRETS REVEALED *Fred Reinfeld*	2.00
CHESS STRATEGY — An Expert's Guide *Fred Reinfeld*	2.00
CHESS TACTICS FOR BEGINNERS *edited by Fred Reinfeld*	2.00
CHESS THEORY & PRACTICE *Morry & Mitchell*	2.00
CHILDBIRTH WITH HYPNOSIS *William S. Kroger, M.D.*	2.00
COIN COLLECTING FOR BEGINNERS *Burton Hobson & Fred Reinfeld*	2.00
CONCENTRATION—A Guide to Mental Mastery *Mouni Sadhu*	2.00
CONVERSATION MADE EASY *Elliot Russell*	1.00
CULPEPER'S HERBAL REMEDIES *Dr. Nicholas Culpeper*	2.00
CYBERNETICS WITHIN US *Y. Saparina*	3.00
DOCTOR PSYCHO-CYBERNETICS *Maxwell Maltz, M.D.*	2.50
DOG TRAINING MADE EASY & FUN *John W. Kellogg*	2.00
DREAMS & OMENS REVEALED *Fred Gettings*	2.00
DR. LINDNER'S SPECIAL WEIGHT CONTROL METHOD	1.00
DYNAMIC THINKING *Melvin Powers*	1.00
ENCYCLOPEDIA OF MODERN SEX & LOVE TECHNIQUES *R. Macandrew*	2.00
EXAM SECRET *Dennis B. Jackson*	1.00
EXTRASENSORY PERCEPTION *Simeon Edmunds*	2.00
FAST GOURMET COOKBOOK *Poppy Cannon*	2.50
FORTUNE TELLING WITH CARDS *P. Foli*	2.00
GAYELORD HAUSER'S NEW GUIDE TO INTELLIGENT REDUCING	3.00
GOULD'S GOLD & SILVER GUIDE TO COINS *Maurice Gould*	2.00
GREATEST POWER IN THE UNIVERSE *U. S. Andersen*	4.00

Melvin Powers
SELF-IMPROVEMENT
LIBRARY

Melvin Powers
SELF-IMPROVEMENT
LIBRARY

PSYCHO-CYBERNETICS
A New Technique for Using Your Subconscious Power
by Maxwell Maltz, M.D., F.I.C.S.

Contents:
1. The Self Image: Your Key to a Better Life 2. Discovering the Success Mechanism Within You 3. Imagination—The First Key to Your Success Mechanism 4. Dehypnotize Yourself from False Beliefs 5. How to Utilize the Power of Rational Thinking 6. Relax and Let Your Success Mechanism Work for You 7. You Can Acquire the Habit of Happiness 8. Ingredients of the Success-Type Personality and How to Acquire Them 9. The Failure Mechanism: How to Make It Work For You Instead of Against You 10. How to Remove Emotional Scars, or How to Give Yourself an Emotional Face Lift 11. How to Unlock Your Real Personality 12. Do-It-Yourself Tranquilizers That Bring Peace of Mind 13. How to Turn a Crisis into a Creative Opportunity. **268 Pages . . . $2**

A PRACTICAL GUIDE TO SELF-HYPNOSIS
by Melvin Powers

Contents:
1. What You Should Know About Self-Hypnosis 2. What About the Dangers of Hypnosis? 3. Is Hypnosis the Answer? 4. How Does Self-Hypnosis Work? 5. How to Arouse Yourself From the Self-Hypnotic State 6. How to Attain Self-Hypnosis 7. Deepening the Self-Hypnotic State 8. What You Should Know About Becoming an Excellent Subject 9. Techniques for Reaching the Somnambulistic State. 10. A New Approach to Self-Hypnosis When All Else Fails 11. Psychological Aids and Their Function 12. The Nature of Hypnosis **120 Pages . . . $2**

A GUIDE TO RATIONAL LIVING
by Albert Ellis, Ph.D. & Robert A. Harper, Ph.D.

Contents:
1. How Far Can You Go With Self-Analysis? 2. You Feel as You Think 3. Feeling Well by Thinking Straight 4. What Your Feelings Really Are 5. Thinking Yourself Out of Emotional Disturbances 6. Recognizing and Attacking Neurotic Behavior 7. Overcoming the Influences of the Past 8. How Reasonable is Reason? 9. The Art of Never Being Desperately Unhappy 10. Tackling Dire Needs for Approval 11. Eradicating Dire Fears of Failure 12. How to Stop Blaming and Start Living 13. How to Be Happy Though Frustrated 14. Controlling Your Own Destiny 15. Conquering Anxiety 16. Conquering Self-discipline 17. Rewriting Your Personal History 18. Accepting Reality 19. Overcoming Inertia and Becoming Creatively Absorbed **208 Pages . . . $2**

A GUIDE TO SUCCESSFUL MARRIAGE
by Albert Ellis, Ph.D. & Robert A. Harper, Ph.D.

Contents:
1. Modern Marriage: Hotbed of Neurosis 2. Factors Causing Marital Disturbance 3. Gauging Marital Compatibility 4. Problem Solving in Marriage 5. Can We Be Intelligent About Marriage? 6. Love or Infatuation? 7. To Marry or Not To Marry 8. Sexual Preparation for Marriage 9. Impotence in the Male 10. Frigidity in the Female 11. Sex "Excess" 12. Controlling Sex Impulses 13. Nonmonogamous Desires 14. Communication in Marriage 15. Children 16. In-laws 17. Marital Incompatibility Versus Neurosis 18. Divorce 19. Succeeding in Marriage 20. Selected Readings **304 Pages . . . $2**

HOW YOU CAN HAVE CONFIDENCE & POWER
by Les Giblin

Contents:
1. Your Key to Success and Happiness 2. How to Use the Basic Secret for Influencing Others 3. How to Cash in on Your Hidden Assets 4. How to Control the Actions & Attitudes of Others 5. How You Can Create a Good Impression on Other People 6. Techniques for Making & Keeping Friends 7. How to Use Three Big Secrets for Attracting People 8. How to Make the Other Person Feel Friendly—Instantly 9. How You Can Develop Skill in Using Words 10. The Technique of "White Magic" 11. How to Get Others to See Things Your Way—Quickly 12. A Simple, Effective Plan of Action That Will Bring You Success and Happiness. **180 Pages . . . $2**

The books listed above can be obtained from your book dealer or directly from Wilshire Book Company. When ordering, please remit 10c per book postage.
Send for our free 224 page illustrated catalog of self-improvement books.

Wilshire Book Company
12015 Sherman Road, No. Hollywood, California 91605

Notes

Notes

Notes

Notes

Notes

Notes

Notes

Notes

Notes

Notes

Notes

Notes

Notes

Notes

Notes

Notes

Notes

Notes

Notes

Notes

Notes